A Roadmap to Accounting for Environmental Obligations and Asset Retirement Obligations

Other Publications in Deloitte's Roadmap Series

Roadmaps are available on these topics:

Asset Acquisitions (2017)

Carve-Out Transactions (2018)

Common-Control Transactions (2016)

Consolidation — Identifying a Controlling Financial Interest (2017)

Contracts on an Entity's Own Equity (2017)

Discontinued Operations (2017)

Distinguishing Liabilities From Equity (2017)

Equity Method Investees — SEC Reporting Considerations (2018)

Foreign Currency Transactions and Translations (2017)

Income Taxes (2017)

Leases (2018)

Noncontrolling Interests (2017)

Non-GAAP Financial Measures (2017)

The Preparation of the Statement of Cash Flows (2017)

Pushdown Accounting (2016)

Revenue Recognition (2017)

Segment Reporting (2017)

Share-Based Payment Awards (2017)

Roadmaps on these topics will be available soon:

Business Combinations

Earnings per Share

Equity Method Investments and Joint Ventures

Initial Public Offerings

Contents

Preface

June 2018

To the clients, friends, and people of Deloitte:

The guidance on accounting for environmental obligations and asset retirement obligations (AROs) is unique because of its dependency on the various laws and regulations governing such obligations. Given that dependency, we have created this Roadmap to illustrate and help you navigate the intersection of law and accounting related to environmental obligations and AROs.

The accounting guidance on loss contingencies in ASC 450-20[1] provides the framework for the accounting for environmental obligations under ASC 410-30. The accounting requirements for environmental obligations under ASC 410-30 are generally based on federal and state environmental laws in the United States. Accordingly, this Roadmap provides an overview of some of the applicable state and federal environmental laws in the United States and describes the application of the accounting guidance within this legal framework.

Unlike environmental obligations, AROs typically arise as a result of state laws and asset-specific operating permits. This Roadmap describes the accounting requirements for AROs in ASC 410-20 and includes a discussion of certain relevant industry considerations within the context of the laws and regulations governing AROs for various industries.

> Subscribers to the Deloitte Accounting Research Tool (DART) may access any interim updates to this publication by selecting the document from the "Roadmaps" tab on DART's home page. If a "Summary of Changes Since Issuance" displays, subscribers can view those changes by clicking the related links or by opening the "active" version of the Roadmap.

Note that while this Roadmap is intended to be a helpful resource, it is not a substitute for consulting with Deloitte professionals on complex accounting questions and transactions.

We hope that you find this publication to be a valuable resource when considering the guidance on environmental obligations and AROs.

Sincerely,

Deloitte & Touche LLP

---

[1] For a list of the titles of standards and other literature referred to in this publication, see Appendix C. For a list of abbreviations used in this publication, see Appendix D.

Acknowledgments

Dennis Howell and Andrew Hubacker oversaw the development of this publication. They are grateful for the thought leadership and technical contributions of James Barker, Matt Harold, Kevin Moore, Nick Tricarichi, Jamie Varkey, and Teal White.

Dennis and Andrew also wish to extend their appreciation to Teri Asarito, Amy Davidson, Geri Driscoll, David Eisenberg, David Frangione, and Michael Lorenzo for delivering the first-class editorial and production effort that we have come to rely on.

Contacts

If you have questions about the information in this publication, please contact any of the following Deloitte professionals:

Dennis Howell
Partner
Audit & Assurance
Deloitte & Touche LLP
+1 203 761 3478
dhowell@deloitte.com

Andrew Hubacker
Partner
Audit & Assurance
Deloitte & Touche LLP
+1 313 394 5362
ahubacker@deloitte.com

Jamie Varkey
Specialist Leader
Risk & Financial Advisory
Deloitte Transactions and
Business Analytics LLP
+1 214 840 7944
jamivarkey@deloitte.com

Teal White
Specialist Master
Risk & Financial Advisory
Deloitte Transactions and
Business Analytics LLP
+1 214 840 1636
tewhite@deloitte.com

Matt Harold
Manager
Risk & Financial Advisory
Deloitte Transactions and
Business Analytics LLP
+1 713 982 2610
mharold@deloitte.com

Chapter 1 — Overview

An environmental remediation liability is a legal obligation to remove or remediate pollution or contaminants from environmental media such as soil, groundwater, sediment, and surface water. Environmental remediation liabilities can arise in many ways. For example, they may result from the operation, retirement, closing, or mere ownership of a facility (currently or in the past) at or near a contaminated site. The FASB's guidance on accounting for environmental remediation liabilities is codified in ASC 410-30.

An ARO is a legal obligation associated with the retirement of a tangible long-lived asset that results from the acquisition, construction, development, or normal operation of a long-lived asset. The FASB's guidance on accounting for AROs is codified in ASC 410-20.

The guidance in ASC 410-30 is based on federal environmental laws and regulations in the United States. Specifically, the guidance is based largely on the Comprehensive Environmental Response, Compensation, and Liability Act of 1980 (CERCLA or the "Superfund") and the corrective action provisions of the Resource Conservation and Recovery Act of 1976 (RCRA). Since certain aspects of the accounting guidance for environmental remediation liabilities refer specifically to both statutes, we believe that it is beneficial for entities to understand the requirements of each of those laws before applying the accounting guidance in ASC 410-30. Accordingly, this Roadmap's discussion of environmental remediation liabilities is designed to provide both an overview of the legal and regulatory framework of environmental obligations, primarily in the United States (see Chapter 2), and a detailed explanation of the FASB's guidance on accounting for environmental remediation liabilities (see Chapter 3).

In ASC 410-20, the guidance on AROs is predicated on the existence of a legal obligation to retire an asset, which, in accordance with the definition of a legal obligation in ASC 410-20-20, can arise from "an existing or enacted law, statute, ordinance, or written or oral contract or by legal construction of a contract under the doctrine of promissory estoppel." However, unlike environmental remediation liabilities (which are largely governed by comprehensive federal statutes and regulations), AROs in the United States are largely the result of state statutes and regulations and typically arise as a result of asset-specific operating permits. Accordingly, our discussion of AROs first addresses the accounting framework in ASC 410-20 (see Chapter 4), including relevant interpretive accounting and financial reporting guidance. The Roadmap then gives an overview of certain legal and regulatory requirements and certain specific accounting considerations related to various industry- and asset-specific AROs (see Chapter 5).

In Chapters 2 and 5 of this Roadmap, much of the content related to environmental remediation liabilities and AROs is adapted from EPA and other environmental literature. We have provided numerous links in the text, as well as a compilation of environmental literature in Appendix B, to direct you to the various sources should you wish to explore the material in greater detail.

1.1   Environmental Remediation Liabilities

An environmental remediation liability is a specific type of contingent liability that arises, typically, from federal, state, and local environmental regulations related to environmental contamination in soil, sediment, groundwater and surface water. These regulations often create a cleanup standard that defines the level of contamination at or above which remedial action must be taken. For example, governmental regulations may define the allowable amount of contamination in drinking water before remediation is required.

In a manner consistent with the guidance in ASC 450-20, an environmental remediation liability should be recognized when it is probable that such a liability has been incurred and the amount of the liability can be reasonably estimated. The concepts of "probable" and "reasonably estimable" are based on the framework outlined in ASC 450-20. ASC 410-30 provides additional guidance on how to apply these concepts in the context of some of the unique characteristics of the environmental remediation statutes and regulations in the United States.

An environmental remediation liability generally does not become fixed or determinable at a specific point in time. Rather, the existence and amount of an environmental remediation liability become determinable over a continuum of events and activities. That is, the activities associated with environmental remediation are often dynamic (i.e., they progress through stages in which both the remediation requirements and the ability to estimate costs change). For example, a typical environmental remediation process consists of (1) identifying entities that may have contributed to the contamination, (2) performing a remedial investigation to identify possible remedies, (3) conducting a feasibility study to evaluate the cost and viability of the various remedies identified, (4) completing the selected remedy, and (5) operating and maintaining the site after completion of the remedy. Therefore, there is often uncertainty about whether and, if so, when a legal obligation for environmental remediation has been incurred. In situations involving contaminated drinking water, many types of groundwater remediation can be performed with varying degrees of success and efficiency. In addition, groundwater contamination can spread at different concentrations across an often imprecisely defined area. Each of these factors leads to uncertainty, which can affect the estimation of costs associated with groundwater remediation.

Not all environmental remediation activities result in environmental obligations that are subject to the guidance in ASC 410-30. Specifically, in accordance with ASC 410-30-15-3, the following transactions and activities are outside the scope of ASC 410-30:

- "Environmental contamination incurred in the normal operation of a long-lived asset," which is accounted for as an ARO under ASC 410-20. (See Section 1.3 for guidance on determining whether an environmental remediation liability is within the scope of ASC 410-20 or 410-30.)

- "Pollution control costs with respect to current operations or on accounting for costs of future site restoration or closure that are required upon the cessation of operations or sale of facilities."

- "Environmental remediation actions that are undertaken at the sole discretion of management and that are not induced by the threat, by governments or other parties, of litigation or of assertion of a claim or an assessment."

- "Recognizing liabilities of insurance entities for unpaid claims."

- "Natural resource damages and toxic torts."

- "Asset impairment issues."

See Chapter 3 for additional guidance on accounting for environmental remediation obligations under U.S. GAAP.

1.2 Asset Retirement Obligations

An ARO is defined in ASC 410-20-20 as an "obligation associated with the retirement of a tangible long-lived asset." The obligation arises from a legal requirement (i.e., a permit, court order, authorization, or lease) when the construction or operation of an asset results in the need to complete an action upon retirement of the asset. An ARO exists when the obligation to perform the asset retirement activity is unconditional even though there may be uncertainty about whether and, if so, how and when the obligation will ultimately be settled. The following are examples of common AROs:

- Landfill closure and postclosure care.

- Mine reclamation.

- Nuclear decommissioning.

- Oil well plugging and abandonment.

- Abatement of asbestos-containing materials.

- Underground storage tank removal.

See Chapter 4 for additional guidance on accounting for AROs under U.S. GAAP.

1.3 Determining Whether an Environmental Remediation Liability Is Within the Scope of ASC 410-20 or ASC 410-30

An environmental remediation liability may arise in connection with an obligation to retire a tangible long-lived asset. In such situations, the environmental remediation liability may be within the scope of either ASC 410-20 or ASC 410-30 depending on the facts and circumstances. Determining which set of guidance to apply to an environmental remediation liability is critical because there are significant differences between ASC 410-20 and ASC 410-30, as summarized in the table below.

Concept	Accounting Under ASC 410-20	Accounting Under ASC 410-30
Recognizing a liability		
Timing	When or as incurred (if a reasonable estimate of fair value can be made).	When it is probable that a liability has been incurred and the amount of the liability is reasonably estimable.
Manner	Capitalized as an asset retirement cost. Under ASC 410-20-25-5, the reporting entity recognizes the liability "by increasing the carrying amount of the related long-lived asset by the same amount as the liability."	Expensed. The liability is generally expensed as incurred as a loss contingency. However, environmental remediation costs may be capitalized if certain conditions are met.

(Table continued)

Concept	Accounting Under ASC 410-20	Accounting Under ASC 410-30
Measuring a liability		
Initial measurement	Fair value (discounted). An entity typically measures the fair value of an ARO by using an "expected present value" technique.	Estimated costs to remediate the site (generally undiscounted). Environmental liabilities are generally undiscounted; however, they may be discounted if certain conditions are met.
Subsequent measurement	Changes attributable to the passage of time are accounted for under the interest method. An entity accounts for changes in the timing or amount of expected future cash flows by adjusting the carrying amount of the liability and recording the offset to the related capitalized asset retirement cost.	Continuously update the estimated costs to complete the remediation, with changes accounted for as changes in estimate.
Effects of uncertainty	Uncertainty is factored into the measurement of the fair value of the liability.	Uncertainty is factored into both the recognition and measurement of the liability.

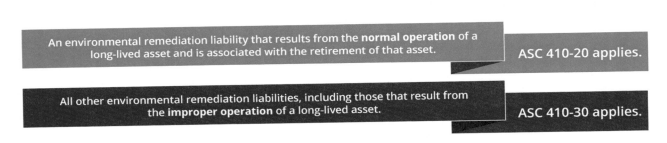

An environmental remediation liability that results from the **normal operation** of a long-lived asset and is associated with the retirement of that asset. **ASC 410-20 applies.**

All other environmental remediation liabilities, including those that result from the **improper operation** of a long-lived asset. **ASC 410-30 applies.**

The scope of ASC 410-20 is limited to those obligations that cannot be realistically avoided, assuming that the asset is operated in accordance with its intended use. Contamination arising from "normal" operations generally is expected or predictable, gradual (or occurring over time), integral to operations, or unavoidable and does not require an immediate response.

If an environmental remediation obligation results from either "improper" operation of an asset or a catastrophic event, it would be subject to the provisions of ASC 410-30 or ASC 450. Contamination arising from improper use of an asset or a catastrophic event is generally unexpected, requires immediate response or reporting, generally could have been controlled or mitigated, and is the result of a failure in equipment or noncompliance with company procedures.

The examples below illustrate differences between environmental remediation liabilities that should be accounted for under ASC 410-20 (Example 1-1) and those that should be accounted for under ASC 410-30 (Example 1-2).

Example 1-1

Environmental Remediation Liability Under ASC 410-20

An entity that operates a nuclear power plant has a legal obligation to decontaminate the site upon the closure of the facility. As stated in the U.S. Nuclear Regulatory Commission's (NRC's) fact sheet on decommissioning nuclear power plants, the obligation is related to decommissioning activities that include, but are not limited to, the "permanent removal of such major components as the reactor vessel, steam generators, large piping systems, pumps, and valves." Because the obligation results from the normal operation of the asset, the obligation should be accounted for under the provisions of ASC 410-20.

Example 1-2

Environmental Remediation Liability Under ASC 410-30

An entity operates a nuclear power plant at which the occurrence of a catastrophic accident results in the contamination of land surrounding the site. Under local and federal laws, the entity is required to remediate the radioactive materials. Because the obligation to remediate the land around the site results from a catastrophic event (i.e., improper operation of the asset), the obligation should be accounted for under the ASC 450/ASC 410-30 probability model.

Chapter 2 — Environmental Regulations

Environmental laws can be derived from a combination of federal, state, and local laws (and, in some instances, international treaties) related to matters such as the protection of the environment and natural resources. For example, environmental laws often pertain to issues such as air, water, or soil pollution; global warming; and the depletion of natural resources, including clean water and fossil fuels. Although the U.S. Environmental Protection Agency (EPA) is the primary environmental regulator in the United States, it does not handle *all* environmental concerns. Some environmental issues are mainly concerns of other federal, tribal, state, or local agencies. The EPA conditionally delegates many environmental programs to the states.

In ASC 410-30, the guidance on accounting for environmental obligations classifies environmental laws into two categories: (1) environmental remediation liability laws and (2) laws intended to control or prevent pollution. Environmental laws within either category can be federal, state, or international.

The remainder of this chapter focuses primarily on some of the major U.S. federal environmental regulations that serve as drivers of environmental remediation liabilities. The sections below begin with a summary of these regulations and continue with an in-depth discussion of the "Superfund" regulation and discussions of state and international considerations.

2.1 Environmental Regulations — Federal

ASC 410-30

05-5 The first kind of environmental law, environmental remediation liability laws, includes individual statutes as well as response provisions in other statutes. The most important of these are the Comprehensive Environmental Response, Compensation, and Liability Act of 1980, as amended by the Superfund Amendments and the Reauthorization Act of 1986, which together are referred to as Superfund, and the corrective action provisions of the Resource Conservation and Recovery Act of 1976. . . .

05-8 Environmental laws of the second kind are intended to control or prevent pollution and are directed at identifying or regulating pollution sources or reducing emissions or discharges of pollutants. There are many statutes that regulate sources of pollution, including the pollution control provisions of the Resource Conservation and Recovery Act of 1976 (solid and hazardous wastes), the Clean Water Act (discharge of pollutants into the waters of the United States and to publicly owned treatment works), and the Clean Air Act (emission of pollutants into the atmosphere). Other examples are the Emergency Planning and Community Right-to-Know Act and the Pollution Prevention Act of 1990.

The following are some of the main federal regulations that serve as drivers of environmental liabilities:

- The Clean Air Act of 1970 (CAA).

- The Clean Water Act of 1972 (CWA).

- The Toxic Substances Control Act of 1976 (TSCA).

- The Resource Conservation and Recovery Act of 1976 (RCRA).

- The Comprehensive Environmental Response, Compensation, and Liability Act of 1980 (CERCLA or "Superfund").

2.1.1   The CAA

The CAA regulates air emissions from both stationary and mobile sources. For example, the law authorizes the EPA to set the National Ambient Air Quality Standards (NAAQS), which protect health and public welfare and regulate emissions of hazardous air pollutants. Congress established much of the basic structure of the CAA in 1970 and made major revisions to the law in 1977 and 1990. The changes were designed to improve the effectiveness of the CAA and target newly recognized air pollution problems such as acid rain and damage to the stratospheric ozone layer. For example, the 1990 CAA Amendments introduced new requirements, including the following:

- Air pollution sources must obtain an operating permit from the state, which would be pursuant to a federally approved program that satisfies the requirements of the CAA.

- Mandates related to the control or reduction of 189 toxic air pollutants emitted by:

  ◦ Major sources emitting 10 tons per year of any one, or 25 tons per year of any combination, of those pollutants.

  ◦ Area sources (i.e., smaller sources such as dry cleaners).

- The establishment of a Chemical Safety Board to investigate accidental releases of chemicals.

For some air pollution problems (e.g., acid rain, ozone layer protection, vehicle emissions, and certain stationary source programs involving common pollutants), the CAA Amendments encourage the use of market-based principles, such as performance-based standards and emissions banking and trading.

For example, in allowance trading, affected sources such as utilities are required to install systems that continuously monitor emissions of sulfur dioxide (SO_2), nitrogen oxides (NO_x), and other related pollutants to track progress and ensure compliance. Entities that reduce their emissions below their held number of allowances may (1) trade allowances with other entities in their system, (2) sell them to other entities on the open market or through EPA auctions, or (3) bank them to cover emissions in future years.

2.1.2   The CWA

The Federal Water Pollution Control Act of 1948 was the first major U.S. law to address water pollution. In 1972, the law was amended and became known as the CWA. The CWA regulates discharges of pollutants into U.S. waters and sets quality standards for surface waters. Under the CWA, it is unlawful for an entity to discharge any pollutant from a point source (i.e., a discrete conveyance such as a pipe or man-made ditch) into navigable waters without a National Pollutant Discharge Elimination System (NPDES) program permit.

2.1.3 The TSCA

The TSCA grants the EPA the authority to mandate reporting, recordkeeping and testing requirements, and restrictions related to chemical substances, mixtures, or both. Chemicals regulated under the TSCA include polychlorinated biphenyls (PCBs), asbestos, radon, and lead-based paint. In 2016, Congress enacted the Frank R. Lautenberg Chemical Safety for the 21st Century Act, which amended the TSCA. The 2016 amendments to the TSCA include the following:

- A mandatory requirement for the EPA to evaluate existing chemicals with clear and enforceable deadlines.

- A new risk-based safety standard.

- Increased public transparency for chemical information.

2.1.4 RCRA

Under RCRA, the EPA is authorized to control hazardous waste "from cradle to grave," which includes the generation, transportation, treatment, storage, and disposal of hazardous waste. In addition, RCRA provides a framework for the management of nonhazardous waste. Since its enactment in 1976, RCRA has been amended twice. In 1984, the Federal Hazardous and Solid Waste Amendments (HSWA) revised RCRA to focus on waste minimization, phasing out land disposal of hazardous waste, and corrective action for releases. The 1986 amendments to RCRA enabled the EPA to address environmental problems that could result from storing petroleum and other hazardous substances in underground tanks.

RCRA encompasses several different program areas to ensure compliance with statutes and regulations in the management of hazardous waste and underground storage tanks. For example, Subtitle D of RCRA pertains to nonhazardous solid waste requirements. Regulations established under Subtitle D ban open dumping of waste and set minimum federal criteria for the operation of municipal waste and industrial waste landfills, including design criteria, location restrictions, financial assurance, corrective action (or cleanup), and closure and postclosure requirements. States assume a lead role in implementing these regulations and may set more stringent requirements than those in Subtitle D. In the absence of an approved state program, the federal requirements apply.

Subtitle C of RCRA pertains to the regulation of hazardous waste. Under Subtitle C, the EPA may authorize states (in lieu of the federal government) to implement key provisions of hazardous waste requirements. If a state program does not exist, the EPA implements the hazardous waste requirements in that state. Subtitle C regulations set criteria for (1) hazardous waste generators, (2) transporters, and (3) treatment, storage, and disposal facilities. The criteria include permit requirements, enforcement, and corrective action or cleanup.

2.1.5 CERCLA or Superfund

CERCLA, also known as Superfund, provides a federal "Superfund" to clean up uncontrolled or abandoned hazardous-waste sites as well as accidents, spills, and other emergency releases of pollutants and contaminants into the environment. Under CERCLA, the EPA is authorized to (1) identify the parties that are potentially responsible for the release of pollutants and contaminants (i.e., potentially responsible parties (PRPs)) and (2) request their cooperation in the cleanup (i.e., a financial contribution toward the cleanup and active participation in the cleanup effort). When PRPs cannot be identified or located, or when they fail to act, the EPA will assume the lead role in conducting the cleanup effort. Once the response action has been completed, the EPA can recover costs from financially viable individuals and companies by using various enforcement tools, such as (1) working with the Department of Justice (DOJ) to pursue the PRPs through the federal court system and (2) assessing penalties on the PRPs. The EPA is authorized to implement CERCLA in all 50 states and U.S. territories. However,

Superfund site identification, monitoring, and response activities in states are coordinated through state environmental protection or waste management agencies.

The Superfund Amendments and Reauthorization Act of 1986 (SARA) incorporated various site-specific amendments, definitions, clarifications, and technical requirements within CERCLA, including additional enforcement authorities, settlement provisions, and criminal sanctions for blatant violations. Title III of SARA is the Emergency Planning and Community Right-to-Know Act (EPCRA). EPCRA was designed to help protect communities from chemical hazards to public health, safety, and the environment. The Act requires hazardous chemical emergency planning by federal, state, and local governments; Indian tribes; and private industry. Under EPCRA, private industry is required to report to federal, state, and local governments on its storage, use, and release of hazardous chemicals.

2.1.5.1 RCRA and CERCLA Compared

Of the federal regulations summarized above, RCRA and CERCLA are most commonly viewed as the drivers of the incurrence and recording of an environmental remediation liability. The main difference between the two acts is that RCRA addresses the management of solid and hazardous waste at current operating facilities, while CERCLA focuses on the management and remediation of abandoned, nonoperating sites that are contaminated with hazardous substances. CERCLA tends to be more complicated since the contamination was caused by a past event and more than one party may bear responsibility.

2.2 Superfund — A Deeper Dive

CERCLA, or Superfund, establishes prohibitions and requirements related to closed and abandoned hazardous waste sites. Under CERCLA, the EPA is authorized to order PRPs to (1) perform remedial actions as necessary or (2) reimburse the Superfund for remedial action costs incurred by the EPA (cost recovery). CERCLA also authorizes PRPs to recover cleanup costs from other PRPs (cost contribution). In addition, CERCLA authorizes the EPA to require restoration of natural resources that have been damaged by the release of hazardous substances or the remediation. The CERCLA remedial action process consists of six steps, as illustrated below and discussed in Sections 2.2.1 through 2.2.6.

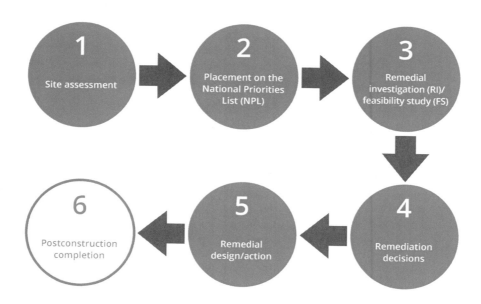

2.2.1 Site Assessment

For a hazardous waste site to be considered a Superfund site, a site assessment must be completed. Superfund site assessments evaluate potential or confirmed releases of hazardous substances that may pose a threat to human health or the environment.

The Superfund site assessment process begins with site discovery or notification of a release or potential release into the environment. The EPA may be notified of hazardous waste activity by citizens, states, tribes, or other environmental programs. After notification, nonfederal sites undergo prescreening for a determination of whether the Superfund site assessment process is appropriate. Sites that are identified as appropriate for the process are assigned a site discovery date and added to the EPA's active CERCLA site inventory.

Once a site is added to the CERCLA site inventory, a site assessment for determining whether the site warrants short-term or long-term cleanup is performed by the EPA or under the environmental program of a state, a tribe, or another federal agency. In site assessments, data are collected so that hazardous waste sites can be identified, evaluated, and ranked on the basis of Hazard Ranking System (HRS) criteria. The HRS is a numerically based screening system that uses information from initial limited investigations to assess the relative potential threat that sites may pose to human health or the environment. Sites with an HRS score below 28.5 generally require no further Superfund remedial attention and receive a "no further remedial action planned" designation. Sites that require additional study are referred to appropriate cleanup programs, including (1) the Emergency Response and Removal Program, (2) the RCRA Corrective Action program, (3) state and tribal cleanup initiatives such as voluntary cleanup programs (VCPs), (4) the Superfund Alternative Approach, and (5) the NPL. Note that only sites listed on the NPL are eligible for Superfund Trust Fund–financed remedial actions. The diagram below illustrates the site assessment process.

Superfund Site Assessment Flow Diagram

---

[1] Preliminary HRS scores are further refined as sites progress through the process. Consequently, a preliminary HRS score greater than 28.5 does not mean that a site would ultimately qualify for the NPL.

[2] For example, RCRA, state voluntary cleanup program.

2.2.2 Placement on the NPL

A site's HRS score determines whether the site is placed on the NPL. Placement is primarily intended to guide the EPA in:

- Determining which sites warrant further investigation to assess the nature and extent of the human health and environmental risks associated with a site.

- Identifying any appropriate CERCLA-financed remedial actions.

- Notifying the public about sites that the EPA believes warrant further investigation.

- Serving notice to PRPs that the EPA may initiate CERCLA-financed remedial action.

Therefore, placement on the NPL does not in itself (1) reflect a judgment of the activities of site owners or operators, (2) require those persons to undertake any action, or (3) assign liability to any person.

Generally, after a site has been placed on the NPL, the EPA will send "notice of liability" letters to entities that are potentially responsible for contaminating the site (see Section 2.2.7).

2.2.3 RI/FS

An RI/FS is performed at a site listed on the NPL. Under the EPA's Enforcement First for Remedial Actions at Superfund Sites policy ("Enforcement First"), the EPA usually asks a PRP to conduct an RI/FS before the agency uses Superfund money. However, if a PRP cannot be located or is delayed in conducting an RI/FS, the EPA can use Superfund money to perform the RI/FS. In some instances, the EPA may conduct its own RI/FS even though an RI/FS is being prepared by a PRP. This may occur, for example, if the EPA is attempting to accelerate the cleanup process by focusing on a smaller area within a larger Superfund site while the PRP is completing the RI/FS for the larger site.

As part of the RI, the PRP, EPA, or both collect data to characterize site conditions, determine the nature of the waste, assess risk to both human health and the environment, and conduct treatability testing to evaluate the potential performance and cost of the treatment technologies being considered. The data are then evaluated in the FS across a range of alternative remedial actions.

The FS has two main components: (1) development and screening of remedial action alternatives and (2) comparison of each alternative that passes screening in a detailed analysis. A range of remedial action alternatives, including cost estimates for each, is developed during the FS as data from the RI site characterization become available. Treatability studies help reduce uncertainties related to cost and performance of treatment alternatives.

2.2.4 Remediation Decisions

The EPA has developed nine criteria for evaluating remedial alternatives to ensure that all important factors are considered in the remedy selection. The criteria are derived from the statutory requirements of CERCLA Section 121, as well as technical and policy considerations. The analysis of remediation alternatives based on the nine criteria comprises two steps: (1) an individual evaluation of each alternative with respect to each criterion and (2) a comparison of options to determine the relative performance of the alternatives and to identify relative advantages and disadvantages. The diagram below depicts the relationship between the nine criteria and the statutory findings of CERCLA.

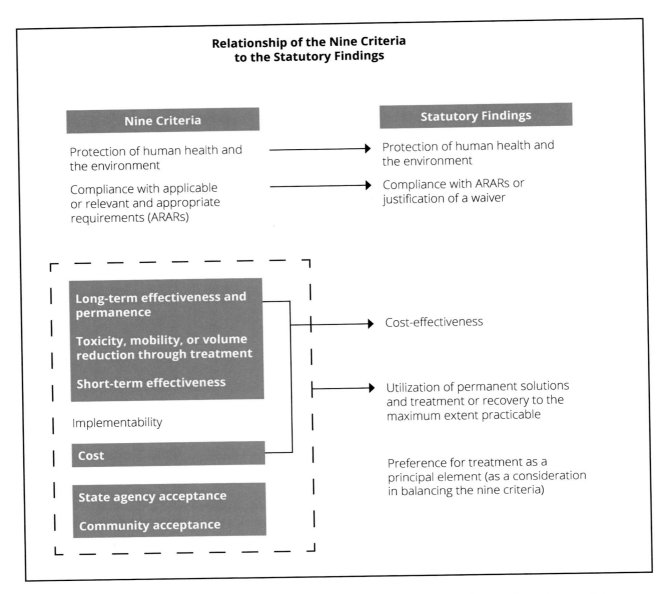

The EPA has also established a two-step remedy selection process, in which a preferred remedial action is presented to the public for comment in a proposed plan. This plan summarizes preliminary conclusions based on information available and considered during the FS. After the receipt and evaluation of public comments on the proposed plan (which may include new information), the EPA will issue a record of decision (ROD) documenting the selected remedy.

The selection of the preferred remedial action (and, ultimately, the remedy specified in the ROD) is based on factors such as the following:

- Environmental media affected (i.e., soil, sediment, groundwater, indoor air).

- Chemical contaminants.

- Remedial objectives.

- Current use of the site.

- Future use of the site.

- Intended cleanup timing.
- Cost.

The types of contaminants of concern (COCs) discovered at a site will depend on current and historical operations and releases, as well as such events at neighboring properties. During environmental remediation projects at industrial facilities such as manufacturing, aerospace, railroad, and oil and gas operations, the most commonly found COCs include the following:

- *Heavy metals* — These troublesome metals include arsenic, chromium, lead, and mercury.
- *Volatile organic compounds (VOCs)* — Chlorinated VOCs, including perchloroethylene (PCE) and trichloroethylene (TCE), are common contaminants. Gasoline-related chemicals such as benzene and methyl tert-butyl ether (MTBE) are also VOCs.
- *Semivolatile organic compounds (SVOCs)* — Polyaromatic hydrocarbons (PAHs) are a subset of SVOCs found in petroleum.
- *Polychlorinated biphenyls (PCBs)* — PCBs were historically used in electrical equipment and are considered persistent organic pollutants because of their longevity.
- *Non-aqueous phase liquids (NAPLs)* — NAPLs are chemicals or mixtures of chemicals (e.g., dry cleaning fluids, fuel oil, and gasoline) that do not dissolve in water. Light non-aqueous phase liquids (LNAPLs) are lighter than water and will float atop the water table. Dense non-aqueous phase liquids (DNAPLs) are heavier than water and will sink in the water column.

As part of the Federal Remediation Technologies Roundtable (FRTR), the EPA helped develop the Remediation Technologies Screening Matrix, a tool to screen for remediation technologies based on some of the factors mentioned above. In addition, the matrix features cost and performance reports developed by members of the FRTR.

The primary driver of the selection of a remediation technique is the type of environmental medium that is affected. Consequently, the discussion of remediation techniques and technologies in Sections 2.2.4.1 through 2.2.4.3 below is organized by the type of affected environmental medium. Further, most of the remedial techniques below also require a term of operations, maintenance, and monitoring (OM&M). See Section 2.2.6.1 for further discussion of the related OM&M considerations.

2.2.4.1 *Soil Remediation*

The most important driver of the remedial technology for contaminated soil is the remedial objective in conjunction with the current and future land use of the site. This is because the soil remediation technologies allow responsible parties to (1) remove the contaminated soil, (2) treat or stabilize the contaminated soil in place, or (3) control exposure to the contaminated soil.

2.2.4.1.1 Soil Removal

Physical removal of chemical contaminants is the most intuitive method for eliminating contaminated soil, and the appropriate technology for doing so is soil excavation. Because excavation physically removes COCs, it is effective for all COCs entrained in the soil matrix; this technique may also remove buried drums of chemicals or other debris that is potentially contaminated. Further, as long as all of the contaminated soil is excavated, excavation can be performed for all future land uses, including those that are most restrictive, such as residential or recreational. However, if a site is currently being used for active operations, soil excavation activities will disrupt operations because of the physical space and access that the excavation machinery requires.

Contaminated soil is excavated with standard construction equipment such as backhoes, and soil may be loaded into dump trucks. The equipment chosen depends on the area's size, the depth of the contamination, and whether access is limited by the presence of buildings or other immovable structures. Although long-arm excavators can reach as deep as 100 feet below ground, excavations are generally limited to shallower depths for reasons such as cost and health and safety. Soil excavation below the water table is possible, but it requires dewatering the excavation (i.e., walling off the contaminated area and pumping out the water). If the pumped water comes into contact with the contaminated soil, the water will most likely require treatment before disposal, which is an additional cost. Deep excavations also typically require shoring[3] to (1) keep the excavation open for collection of postremediation confirmation samples and (2) ensure workers' health and safety.

Once the contaminated soil has been excavated, responsible parties have the following options:

- *Transporting the soil to a licensed landfill for disposal* — Costs of this alternative include equipment and labor for excavation, transportation and disposal fees, and, potentially, additional taxes. Since the excavated and disposed-of soil must be replaced on-site, backfill material and vegetation are additional cost considerations.

- *Treating the soil on- or off-site* — Treated soil may be disposed of at a licensed landfill or returned to the site for use as backfill. To reduce disposal costs, which are higher when hazardous waste is transported and disposed of, a responsible party may elect to treat soil before disposing of it at a landfill. Costs of this alternative, which may be more cost-effective than the transportation and disposal of hazardous waste, include the equipment and labor required for excavation, as well as the treatment, transportation, disposal, backfill, and restoration (e.g., vegetation or pavement). See Section 2.2.4.1.2 below for a discussion of the various soil treatment options.

Excavation is commonly used when in situ (i.e., "in place") treatment methods are too slow or expensive. Because of its effectiveness in removing all contaminated soil, excavation can also be used when unrestricted land use (e.g., residential) is required by a regulator or desired by the property owner. Off-site disposal is often the fastest method for removing high levels of contamination that pose an immediate risk to human health or the environment. Excavation is also a cost-effective approach for removing small amounts of contaminated soil. Finally, there are no long-term OM&M activities related to excavation since it eliminates the contamination and also removes the source of the contamination from underlying groundwater.

2.2.4.1.2 Soil Treatment and Stabilization

When soil excavation is not feasible because of overlying buildings or is impracticable because of the depth or large area of contamination, in situ treatment and stabilization may be effective. In situ technologies involve the application of chemical, biological, or physical processes to soil to degrade, remove, or immobilize contaminants without removing the bulk soil. Compared with excavation and ex situ treatment (i.e., treatment after excavation), these technologies offer several benefits, such as addressing deep contamination and generally costing less.

In situ treatment technologies include the following:

- *Soil vapor extraction* — A vacuum is applied to unsaturated zone soil to induce the controlled flow of air and remove VOCs and some SVOCs from the soil.

- *Air sparging* — Air is injected through a contaminated saturated zone to remove VOCs and SVOCs by volatilization.

---

[3] Shoring is the provision of a support system for trench faces used to prevent movement of soil, underground utilities, roadways, and foundations.

- *Soil washing* — Contaminants absorbed into fine soil particles are separated from bulk soil in a water-based system on the basis of particle size. Soil and wash water are then mixed in a tank or other treatment unit and are usually separated by means of gravity settling.

- *Bioremediation* — Microorganisms are used to degrade organic contaminants in soil, groundwater, sludge, and solids. The microorganisms break down the contaminants by either using them as an energy source or cometabolizing them with an energy source.

- *In situ chemical reduction* — A reductant or reductant-generating material is placed in the subsurface to convert toxic organic compounds into potentially nontoxic or less toxic compounds. The technology uses adsorption or precipitation to immobilize metals, and it degrades nonmetallic oxyanions.

- *In situ oxidation* — This technology involves reduction/oxidation ("redox") reactions that chemically convert hazardous compounds to nonhazardous or less toxic compounds that are more stable, less mobile, or inert.

- *In situ thermal treatment* — Such treatment includes many methods and combinations of techniques for applying heat to polluted soil, groundwater, or both. The heat destroys or volatilizes organic chemicals, and the gases are extracted through collection wells for capture and cleanup in a treatment unit.

- *Solidification* — This technology encapsulates waste to form a solid material, coats the waste with low-permeability materials to restrict contaminant migration, or both. Solidification can occur as a result of either mechanical processes or a chemical reaction between a waste and binding reagents, such as cement, kiln dust, or lime/fly ash.

The time required for cleanup depends on the technique selected, the nature and extent of contaminated soil, and the area of contamination. In addition, regulatory agencies typically require a postremediation monitoring period to verify the efficacy of the remedy. As a result, OM&M activities would be expected components of a soil treatment remediation system.

2.2.4.2 *Groundwater Remediation*

The most important factor determining the selection of a remedial technology for contaminated groundwater is the remedial objective. Objectives can be a combination of the following:

- Preventing ingestion of groundwater whose contaminant levels exceed drinking water standards (either state-enumerated standards or EPA-regulated maximum contaminant levels (MCLs)).

- Preventing contact with, or inhalation of, VOCs from contaminated groundwater.

- Restoring groundwater aquifers to predisposal or prerelease conditions.

- Preventing migration of contaminated groundwater off-site.

When assessing these potential remedial objectives, the responsible party must also consider the current and future use of the groundwater. If groundwater is currently being used for drinking water or will be used in such a way in the future, the groundwater remediation technology must be robust enough to restore the groundwater quality to drinking water standards. However, if the groundwater is *not* used for potable water purposes, and other sources of drinking water are provided to the surrounding community, some other remedial alternatives may be available. These factors are important because with the many groundwater remediation technologies available, responsible parties may elect to (1) remove and treat the contaminated groundwater, (2) treat the contaminated groundwater in place, (3) contain the contaminated groundwater, or (4) control exposure to contaminated soil and groundwater. As discussed below, groundwater can be treated ex situ or in situ.

2.2.4.2.1 Ex Situ Groundwater Treatment

Pump-and-treat systems are among the most common treatment technologies used to remove contaminated groundwater. Groundwater is pumped from extraction wells to an aboveground treatment system that removes the contaminants. Once the groundwater is extracted from the groundwater-bearing unit or aquifer, selection of a treatment technology or technologies will depend on the COCs found in the water. A treatment system may consist of a single cleanup method; however, treatment often requires several methods if the groundwater contains multiple types of contaminants or high concentrations of a single contaminant.

Commonly used ex situ groundwater treatment methods include the following:

- *Air stripping* — This method involves the mass transfer of VOCs from water to air. For groundwater remediation, the process is typically conducted in a packed tower or an aeration tank.

- *Liquid phase carbon adsorption* — Groundwater is pumped through a series of vessels containing activated carbon to which dissolved contaminants are adsorbed. When the concentration of contaminants in the effluent from the bed exceeds a certain level, the carbon can be (1) regenerated in place, (2) removed and regenerated at an off-site facility, or (3) removed and disposed of.

- *Precipitation/flocculation and sedimentation* — This process removes metals from groundwater, typically through the use of precipitation with hydroxides, carbonates, or sulfides. Generally, the precipitating agent is added to water in a rapid-mixing tank along with flocculating agents such as alum, lime, or various iron salts. The mixture then flows to a flocculation chamber that agglomerates particles, which are separated from the liquid phase in a sedimentation chamber. Filtration or other physical processes may follow.

- *Filtration* — This method isolates solid particles by running a fluid stream through a porous medium. The chemicals are not destroyed; they are merely concentrated, making reclamation possible.

- *Ion exchange* — Toxic ions are removed from the aqueous phase in an exchange with relatively innocuous ions held by the ion exchange material. Modern ion exchange resins consist of synthetic organic materials containing ionic functional groups to which exchangeable ions are attached. Other ion exchange materials include clays, zeolites, and peat derivatives. They can be tailored to show selectivity toward specific ions. All metallic elements that are present as soluble species, either anionic or cationic, can be removed by ion exchange.

Note that pump-and-treat systems may also be used to "contain" the contaminant plume. By pumping contaminated water to the surface, a pump-and-treat system controls the movement of contaminated groundwater, preventing the continued expansion of the contaminated zone.

2.2.4.2.2 In Situ Groundwater Treatment

The main advantage of in situ treatment is that groundwater can be treated without being brought to the surface, thus resulting in significant cost savings. However, in situ processes generally require longer periods, and there is less certainty about the uniformity of treatment because of the variability in aquifer characteristics and difficulty in verifying the efficacy of the process. Depending on the site and contamination characteristics, in situ chemical treatment may include (1) injection of reactive chemicals into subsurface soils or aquifers or (2) installation of a permeable chemical treatment wall across the groundwater flow path. Other in situ technologies include thermal treatment, bioremediation, and phytoremediation.

In situ treatments use the physical properties of the contaminants or the contaminated medium to destroy the contamination. In situ groundwater treatment technologies include the following:

- *Air sparging* — Air injected through a contaminated aquifer traverses horizontally and vertically in channels through the soil column, creating an underground stripper that removes contaminants by volatilization. This injected air helps flush the contaminants up into the unsaturated zone, where a vapor extraction system is usually implemented to remove the generated vapor phase contamination.

- *Chemical oxidation* — Chemical oxidants are used to convert hazardous contaminants to nonhazardous or less toxic compounds that are more stable, less mobile, or inert. Peroxide, ozone, and permanganate are some of the most commonly used chemical oxidants. These oxidants have been capable of achieving high treatment efficiencies (e.g., greater than 90 percent) for unsaturated aliphatic compounds (e.g., TCE) and aromatic compounds (e.g., benzene), with very fast reaction rates (90 percent destruction in minutes).

- *Thermal treatment* — Steam is forced into an aquifer through injection wells to vaporize VOCs and SVOCs. Vaporized components rise to the unsaturated zone, where they are removed by vacuum extraction and then treated. Hot water or steam injection is typically of short or medium duration, lasting a few weeks to several months.

- *Bioremediation* — Indigenous or inoculated microorganisms (i.e., fungi, bacteria, and other microbes) degrade (metabolize) organic contaminants found in soil or groundwater. "Enhanced bioremediation" attempts to accelerate the natural biodegradation process by providing nutrients, electron acceptors, and competent degrading microorganisms that may otherwise limit the rapid conversion of contamination organics to innocuous end products.

- *Phytoremediation* — Plants are used to remove, transfer, stabilize, and destroy organic and inorganic contamination in groundwater. Phytoremediation mechanisms include enhanced rhizosphere biodegradation, hydraulic control, phytodegradation, and phytovolatilization.

These in situ treatment technologies may be combined with pump-and-treat systems to enhance the mobility of contaminants, thus increasing the recovery of subsurface contamination.

A permeable chemical treatment wall, or permeable reactive barrier (PRB), is a physical wall created below ground that contains reactive materials within the wall filling. Groundwater can flow through a PRB, and the reactive chemicals that make up the wall trap harmful contaminants or reduce their harmfulness. The treated groundwater then flows out of the other side of the wall. It may take many years for PRBs to clean up contaminated groundwater. A PRB is generally used as part of a "treatment train" rather than as a stand-alone remedy. For example, a PRB may act as a polishing technology after active source removal such as physical removal, thermal treatment, soil vapor extraction, or bioremediation.

2.2.4.2.3 Monitored Natural Attenuation

Natural attenuation is an in situ method that relies on natural processes to decrease or "attenuate" concentrations of contaminants in groundwater. Responsible parties monitor the groundwater conditions to ensure that the natural processes are working; therefore, the remediation process is referred to as monitored natural attenuation (MNA). The degradation of chemicals can be effected by a range of physical and biological processes. For example, naturally occurring microorganisms can break down target contaminants, such as fuels and chlorinated solvents, into less toxic or nontoxic substances. Physical mechanisms, including sorption, dispersion, dilution, and volatilization, may also work to remediate the groundwater.

Since MNA is most effective at a site where the source of contamination has been removed, it is most often combined with other soil and groundwater remediation technologies. Further, MNA may take several years, or even decades, to clean up a site. The actual cleanup time will depend on the size of the groundwater plume, the contaminant levels, and the chemistry of the groundwater to support bioremediation processes. As with other treatment technologies, when a party estimates the duration of MNA for cost estimation purposes, it should reference objective evidence related to remaining concentrations and observable trends. The EPA and states have published robust guidance and documentation about the evidence that should be collected when the efficacy of MNA is evaluated.

2.2.4.2.4 Groundwater Containment

Proper design allows groundwater extraction within pump-and-treat systems to serve as hydraulic containment. The extraction wells capture contaminated water for treatment and disposal, thereby preventing further migration of contaminated water downgradient. Other remedial technologies rely on physical containment of the groundwater.

Subsurface barrier walls (often referred to as "slurry walls" or "cut-off walls") aim to (1) prevent further migration of contaminant plumes, (2) divert contaminated groundwater from the drinking water intake, (3) divert uncontaminated groundwater flow, and (4) provide a barrier for the groundwater treatment system. Slurry walls consist of a mixture of soil, bentonite clay, and water that is poured into trenches as a "slurry." Other construction technologies include subsurface sheet pile walls (made of materials such as steel, precast concrete, and aluminum) and jet grouting, which injects a grout mixture at high velocities directly into the pore spaces of the soil or rock. The grout replaces and mixes the soil, creating a homogenous mass.

Slurry walls can be constructed in various configurations to manipulate the flow of groundwater. A barrier wall can be keyed into a low-permeability layer, such as underlying bedrock or clay, or it can be hanging in such a way that the wall does not extend into a low-permeability material. Hanging walls are typically used for containing floating contaminants (e.g., LNAPLs) or deflecting the flow of groundwater. Similarly, the aerial geography of slurry walls can be (1) configured to fully encapsulate the source material on all sides or (2) aligned along the downgradient extent of the contaminated plume to prevent migration. Slurry walls are used in conjunction with groundwater pump-and-treat systems to collect contaminated groundwater, and a low-permeability cap on top of the slurry wall can be used to eliminate infiltration into the wall.

2.2.4.2.5 Controlling Exposure to Contaminated Soil and Groundwater

For contaminants to pose a risk to human health or the environment, there must be (1) a source of chemical release, (2) a human or ecological receptor that is potentially exposed to the released chemicals, and (3) an environmental exposure pathway connecting the source and the receptor(s). If any one of these elements is absent, the exposure pathways are incomplete, and there is no risk. One technique for remediating contaminated soil and groundwater is elimination of the exposure pathway through the use of engineering controls, institutional controls, or both.

Engineering controls include various engineered and constructed physical barriers (e.g., soil caps, subsurface venting systems, subsurface walls, mitigation barriers, and fences) that contain or prevent exposure to property contamination. In contrast, institutional controls are administrative or legal instruments (e.g., deed restrictions or notices, easements, covenants, and zoning) that impose restrictions on the use of contaminated property or resources. Although institutional controls are often found without engineering controls, institutional controls are usually an integral part of engineering control protectiveness. The most common institutional controls for environmental remediation projects (e.g., deed restrictions or notices, covenants) (1) provide information or notification about residual contamination that may remain on a property and (2) identify engineering controls such as soil caps, mitigation barriers, or fencing, which are intended to restrict access and exposure to contamination and eliminate further migration of contamination.

With respect to soil and groundwater remediation, engineering and institutional controls are more cost-effective than removal and treatment technologies. However, because a remedy's effectiveness depends on whether engineering or institutional controls are in place and in good condition, these techniques involve long-term OM&M activities. For engineering controls, OM&M activities may include routine inspections of soil caps, fences, or slurry walls, as well as maintenance when damage or wear is identified. For institutional controls, OM&M activities may include routine inspections to verify that (1) the land at issue is being used commercially or industrially rather than residentially or agriculturally and (2) the groundwater is not being used for drinking.

2.2.4.3 *Sediment Remediation*

Contaminated sediment is soil, sand, organic matter, or other minerals accumulated on the bottom of a water body that contain contaminants at levels that may adversely affect human health or the environment. Contamination sources include (1) direct pipeline or outfall discharges to a water body from industrial facilities, (2) chemical spills that migrate to a water body, (3) surface runoff or erosion of soil from contaminated sources on land, and (4) up-welling of contaminated groundwater or NAPLs into a water body. Remediation of contaminated sediment tends to be costly and logistically complex for the following reasons:

- Water bodies may be affected by several sources of historical contamination.
- Contamination is often diffuse, and sites are often large.
- The aquatic environment is dynamic, and it is difficult to understand the various effects on sediment movement.
- Logistics associated with conducting physical remediation activities are frequently complicated.
- Many sediment sites contain ecologically valuable resources or legislatively protected species or habitats.
- Several riparian landowners may be affected and involved in the process.
- Navigational abilities must be considered on larger waterways.

2.2.4.3.1 Dredging and Excavation

The two most common means of removing contaminated sediment from a water body are dredging (for submerged sediment) and excavation (for sediment from which water has been diverted or drained).

Such removal is effective for source control (i.e., removal of hot spots), but it could be less effective for overall risk reduction because of resuspension and residual contamination. Both methods typically require transporting the sediment to a location for treatment, disposal, or both. They also frequently include treatment of water from dewatered sediment before discharge to an appropriate receiving water body. Key components for an entity to evaluate in deciding whether to use dredging or excavation as a cleanup method include sediment removal, transport, staging, treatment (any necessary pretreatment or treatment of water and sediment), and disposal (liquids and solids).

Dredging and excavation are usually more complex and costly than other sediment remediation techniques because of (1) the removal activities themselves; (2) the need for transport, staging, treatment (if necessary), and disposal of the dredged sediment; and (3) the accommodation of equipment maneuverability and portability or site access.

2.2.4.3.2   In Situ Techniques

The most common in situ sediment remediation techniques include in situ treatment and capping.

In situ sediment treatment mixes an amendment into sediment (1) passively through natural biological processes, such as bioturbation, or (2) actively through mechanical means. Amendment materials are used to transform, degrade, stabilize, or solidify contaminated sediment and may include components that are biological (e.g., cultured microorganisms), chemical (e.g., zerovalent iron), or physical (e.g., clay and concrete). In situ treatment technologies can reduce risk in environmentally sensitive ecosystems such as wetlands and submerged aquatic vegetation habitats, where sediment removal or containment by capping might be harmful. Treatment works to reduce concentrations of freely dissolved chemicals that are exposed to organisms or that may be mobilized and transferred from sediment to the overlying water column.

Capping involves the placement of a subaqueous covering or cap of clean material over contaminated sediment to mitigate the risks posed by the sediments. Caps are generally constructed of granular material (e.g., clean sand or gravel). A more complex cap design can include (1) geotextiles to aid in layer separation or geotechnical stability, (2) amendments to enhance protectiveness, or (3) additional layers to protect and maintain the cap's integrity or enhance its habitat characteristics. Depending on the contaminants and sediment environment, a cap is designed to reduce risk by (1) physically isolating the contaminated sediment, (2) stabilizing the contaminated sediment to reduce transport downgradient, and (3) chemically isolating the contaminated sediment to reduce dissolution into the water column. A cap can be used after partial removal of contaminated sediment or as a stand-alone technique.

2.2.4.3.3   Monitored Natural Recovery

The National Research Council defines monitored natural recovery (MNR) as a remediation practice that uses natural processes to protect the environment and receptors from unacceptable exposures to contaminants. These processes may include physical, biological, and chemical mechanisms that act together to reduce the risks posed by the contaminants. Enhanced MNR (EMNR) involves application of materials or amendments to enhance these natural recovery processes (e.g., the addition of a thin-layer cap or a carbon amendment). The caps enhance ongoing natural recovery processes while minimizing effects on the surrounding aquatic environment. MNR and EMNR can be used alone or in combination with active remediation technologies to meet remedial objectives.

MNR usually involves acquisition of information about ongoing physical, chemical, and biological processes over time to confirm that these risk-reduction processes are occurring. Consequently, MNR is similar to the MNA remedy used for groundwater; however, while degradation or transformation of contaminants is usually the major attenuating process for contaminated groundwater, these processes often work too slowly for sediment remediation to occur in a reasonable time frame. Therefore, physical removal (dredging or excavation) and physical isolation (capping) are the most frequently used processes for sediment remediation. Two key advantages of MNR are its relatively low implementation cost and its noninvasive nature. Two key limitations of MNR are that it generally leaves contaminants in place and may reduce risks more slowly than active remedies do.

2.2.5   Remedial Design/Action

During the remedial design stage, the technical specifications for the selected remedy are designed. Once the design has been finalized, actual construction and implementation of the remedial action are conducted. If PRPs have been identified, the remedial design and action are conducted and funded by the PRPs, with oversight by the EPA and other regulatory agencies if applicable.

2.2.6 Postconstruction Completion

Postconstruction activities ensure that Superfund response actions provide long-term protection of human health and the environment. Such activities include OM&M, long-term response actions (LTRAs), institutional controls, five-year reviews, and site deletion from the NPL.

2.2.6.1 OM&M

With the exception of removal activities, in which contaminated soil or sediment has been excavated and the site has been restored to prerelease conditions, all remedial technologies require a period of OM&M. For example, after a groundwater pump-and-treat system is constructed, the actual remediation process is the long-term operation of that system, along with contemporaneous monitoring of the groundwater quality to evaluate whether the system is remediating the groundwater. In addition, if a landfill or other source of soil contamination is capped, the cap must be inspected and repaired over time so that the remedy remains protective of human health and the environment. OM&M measures may also include maintaining institutional controls.

The purpose of OM&M is to ensure that the selected remedy is performing as intended. Adequate performance of OM&M activities over the lifetime of the remedy or project is critical to ensuring that the remedy continues to protect human health and the environment. The table below illustrates activities commonly performed as part of OM&M.

Typical OM&M Activities	
Inspection	• Review sampling records for compliance with discharge permits and deviations. • Observe site conditions such as landscape, drainage, erosion, and integrity of structures and fences. • Inspect wells, piping, treatment facilities, and other mechanical and electrical systems and equipment.
Sampling, monitoring, and analysis	• Sample and monitor leachate, groundwater, and surface water. • Sample gas collection system and air. • Sample influent/effluent of treatment systems.
Routine operations and maintenance	• Operate treatment plants. • Perform site maintenance and repair, including maintenance of cap integrity, drainage systems, roads, and erosion control. • Maintain institutional controls, fencing, site access, and security measures. • Maintain treatment plant, wells, pumping systems, pollution control devices, and other operating mechanical and electrical equipment.
Reporting	• Provide routine reports. • Provide special reports.

For PRP-led remedies, the PRP continues to operate and maintain the remedy during OM&M. However, the EPA has oversight to ensure that OM&M is being performed adequately. The EPA and the applicable state may require the PRP to submit periodic reports, maintain records, and host site visits from the EPA.

For Superfund-financed remedies, CERCLA Section 104 requires states to pay for or ensure payment for all future maintenance. Although the states are responsible for OM&M, the EPA retains responsibility for determining when OM&M is complete and conducting five-year reviews. OM&M activities may continue for decades, and costs for OM&M are considered during the development of the FS and should be included in the cost estimates for remedial alternatives.

Past EPA guidance recommended the general use of a 30-year period of analysis for estimating the present value costs of remedial alternatives during the development of the FS. Current EPA guidance acknowledges that while this may be appropriate in some circumstances and is a commonly made simplifying assumption, the use of a 30-year period of analysis without site-specific considerations is not recommended. Site-specific justification should be provided for the period of analysis selected. As noted above in connection with groundwater MNA, the EPA and state regulatory agencies have published guidance identifying evidence to be used for evaluating the efficacy of remedial actions. Responsible parties may use data analytics and modeling to evaluate groundwater trends and estimate the time it will take for concentrations of COCs to meet remedial standards. With the appropriate amount of supporting data, responsible parties may also use their experience at a similarly situated site that has attained regulatory closure to estimate the OM&M duration. Most importantly, the underlying assumptions should be documented, with reference to authority when applicable. Otherwise, determination of OM&M duration may appear arbitrary. Further, responsible parties may sometimes be required to perform OM&M indefinitely for remedies that contain wastes on-site or include institutional controls.

For remedies involving soil, sediment, or groundwater restoration, OM&M may be terminated with regulatory agency approval if all work is completed, cleanup goals have been achieved, and additional monitoring or institutional controls are unnecessary. The estimated time for completing the work (and therefore the assumed duration of OM&M activities for estimating costs) is a significant judgment that should be substantiated with objectively verifiable data.

2.2.6.2   Long-Term Response Action

Section 435(f)(3) of the U.S. government's National Oil and Hazardous Substances Pollution Contingency Plan (NCP) states, in part:

> For Fund-financed remedial actions involving treatment or other measures to restore ground- or surface-water quality to a level that assures protection of human health and the environment, the operation of such treatment or other measures for a period of up to 10 years after the remedy becomes operational and functional will be considered part of the remedial action.

The 10-year period from the "operational and functional" determination to the start of OM&M is defined as an LTRA. As noted in Section 435(f)(2) of the NCP, a remedy becomes operational and functional at the earlier of (1) "one year after construction is complete" or (2) "when the remedy is determined concurrently by the EPA and the state to be functioning properly and is performing as designed." Section 435(f)(2) further states that the "EPA may grant extensions to the one-year period, as appropriate." The most common LTRA remedies are (1) groundwater pumping and treatment and (2) MNA remedies with objectives of aquifer restoration.

2.2.6.3   Five-Year Reviews

A five-year review (FYR) is a statutory requirement that applies to all remedial actions selected under CERCLA Section 121. Under this mandate, the EPA is required to conduct a review every five years, or more frequently if necessary, of the remedies at Superfund sites where hazardous substances remain at levels that potentially pose an unacceptable risk. Removal actions conducted under CERCLA Section 104 and corrective actions conducted under RCRA are not subject to the FYR requirement; however, EPA regions may conduct FYRs for these or other remedies as policy or at its discretion. FYRs are performed throughout the life of a site until hazardous substances, pollutants, or contaminants no longer remain on site at levels that do not allow for unlimited use and unrestricted exposure.

2.2.6.4 Deletion From the NPL

A site may be deleted from the NPL once all response actions are complete and all cleanup goals have been achieved. The EPA is responsible for processing deletions with concurrence from the state in which the Superfund site is located. Deleted sites may still require FYRs to assess protectiveness. If future site conditions are warranted, additional response actions can be taken through the Superfund Trust Fund or by PRPs. Relisting on the NPL is not necessary, but sites can be restored to the list if extensive response work is required. The EPA can also delete portions of sites that meet deletion criteria.

2.2.7 EPA "Notice of Liability" Letters to PRPs

This section provides further detail on the Superfund process and explains how an entity is identified as a PRP and put on notice.

The nature of PRPs and their potential liability is provided in ASC 410-30-05-15 and 05-16 as follows:

ASC 410-30

05-15 Superfund places liability on the following four distinct classes of responsible parties:

a. Current owners or operators of sites at which hazardous substances have been disposed of or abandoned
b. Previous owners or operators of sites at the time of disposal of hazardous substances
c. Parties that "arranged for disposal" of hazardous substances found at the sites
d. Parties that transported hazardous substances to a site, having selected the site for treatment or disposal.

05-16 This liability is imposed regardless of whether a party was negligent, whether the site was in compliance with environmental laws at the time of the disposal, or whether the party participated in or benefited from the deposit of the hazardous substance. Parties that disposed of hazardous substances many years ago — including the years preceding the enactment of the Comprehensive Environmental Response, Compensation, and Liability Act of 1980 — at sites where there is, was, or may be a release into the environment, may be liable for remediation costs.

When a site has been proposed for inclusion on the NPL, the EPA typically determines which entities fall within the categories listed above before issuing a "notice of liability" letter. After identifying PRPs, the EPA uses "general notice" letters and "special notice" letters to communicate with them.

A general notice letter informs the recipient that it (1) has been identified as a PRP at a Superfund site and (2) may be liable for cleanup costs at the site. The letter explains the process for negotiating the cleanup with the EPA, includes information about the Superfund and the site itself, and may include a request for additional information. General notice letters are typically sent to PRPs early in the process, such as when a site has been proposed for inclusion on the NPL. Upon receiving a general notice letter from the EPA, a PRP should evaluate whether recognition of an environmental remediation liability is required under ASC 410-30. See Section 3.2 for further discussion of the recognition of environmental remediation liabilities.

The EPA issues a special notice letter when it is ready to negotiate with PRPs to clean up a site (i.e., at either the RI/FS stage or the remedial design/remedial action (RD/RA) stage). A special notice letter explains to PRPs why the EPA thinks that they are liable and informs them about the EPA's plans for the site cleanup. The letter also invites parties to participate in negotiations with the EPA on performing future cleanup work and reimbursing the EPA for any site-related costs already incurred. The issuance of a special notice letter triggers a "negotiation moratorium," meaning that the EPA agrees, for a certain period, not to unilaterally order the PRP to conduct the cleanup. Although the EPA generally issues special notice letters to PRPs, it may decide not to do so in the following circumstances:

- Past experience with the PRPs indicate that a settlement is unlikely.

- No PRPs have been identified.

- PRPs lack the resources to do what is needed.

2.2.8 Liability Schemes Under CERCLA

The liability schemes of CERCLA differ from traditional common law and statutory liability schemes. Specifically, under CERCLA, the following three liability schemes may apply:

- *Strict liability* — The government does not need to prove that the defendant was at fault. Rather, the government is required to prove only that the party falls within one of the four categories of PRPs, as described in Section 2.2.7.

- *Retroactive liability* — Parties found responsible are liable even if their actions occurred before CERCLA was enacted.

- *Joint and several liability* — Each PRP is potentially liable for the entire cost of cleanup, and it is the responsibility of the PRPs to allocate shares of liability among themselves.

ASC 410-30 includes the following guidance on liability under CERCLA:

ASC 410-30

Strict Liability

05-17 The courts have interpreted the Comprehensive Environmental Response, Compensation, and Liability Act of 1980 to impose strict liability. Thus, a waste generator that disposed of its waste at approved facilities, in accordance with all then-current requirements, having exercised "due care," would nevertheless be liable. Further, a waste generator that is responsible for a small percentage of the total amount of waste at a site may be held liable for the entire cost of remediating the site.

05-18 Also noteworthy is that wastes need not be hazardous wastes for there to be environmental remediation liability. If the waste generator "arranged for disposal" of wastes containing hazardous substances (at any concentration level and regardless of whether the substances were defined as, or known to be, hazardous at the time of disposal), and a "release" of hazardous substances has or could occur, the waste generator could be subject to environmental remediation liability.

05-20 The possibility of becoming subject to liability for environmental remediation costs associated with past waste disposal practices based on strict liability can affect transactions involving the acquisition or merger of an entity or the purchase of land.

Joint and Several Liability

05-21 Through Environmental Protection Agency initiated legal action, liability under the Comprehensive Environmental Response, Compensation, and Liability Act of 1980 may be joint and several. If a potentially responsible party can prove, however, that the harm is divisible and there is a reasonable basis for apportionment of costs, the potentially responsible party may ultimately be responsible only for its portion of the costs.

05-22 In order to mitigate the potentially harsh effects of the strict, joint and several, and retroactive liability scheme, however, Superfund does permit responsible parties to sue other responsible parties to make them contribute to the cost of the remediation or to recover money spent on remediation.

2.2.9 Superfund Settlement Agreements

As discussed in Section 2.2.7, the EPA issues general notice letters and special notice letters to communicate with PRPs about Superfund liability. A general notice letter puts a PRP on notice that it may be liable for costs associated with the cleanup of a Superfund site. A special notice letter invites a PRP to enter into good-faith negotiations with the EPA. Typically, a PRP has 60 days to provide the EPA with a good-faith offer to do site work or pay for cleanup. If the PRP provides such an offer, the entity generally has an additional 60 days for negotiation. If the PRP does not submit a good-faith offer at the end of the 60 days, the EPA may start the cleanup work or issue a unilateral administrative order requiring the PRP to do the work.

PRPs can enter into various types of Superfund settlement agreements with the EPA. Such settlement agreements are summarized in the table below.

Settlement Agreement Type	Description	Typical Uses	Court Approval Required
Administrative order on consent (AOC)	A legal document that formalizes an agreement between the EPA and one or more PRPs to address some or all of the parties' responsibilities at a site.	• Removal activity (short-term cleanup). • Investigation. • Remedy design work. • Cost recovery when payments are made as part of an agreement for work and for de minimis cash-out payments.	No
Administrative agreement	A legal document that formalizes an agreement between the EPA and one or more PRPs to reimburse the EPA for costs already incurred (cost recovery) or costs to be incurred (cash-out) at a Superfund site.	All types of payment agreements that do not include performance of work.	No
Judicial consent decree	A legal agreement entered into by the United States (through the EPA and the DOJ) and PRPs. A consent decree (CD) is the only settlement type that the EPA can use for the final cleanup phase (remedial action) at a Superfund site.	• Final cleanup. • Recovery of cleanup costs in cost recovery and cash-out settlements. • Performance of removal work or an RI/FS.	Yes
Work agreement	The EPA and a PRP negotiate an agreement (in the form of an AOC or CD) that outlines the work to be done. The term "work agreement" covers a variety of agreements under which the PRP (rather than the EPA) performs the work.	• Site investigations (RI/FS). • Short-term cleanup (removal actions). • Long-term cleanup (RD/RA).	No

(Table continued)

Settlement Agreement Type	Description	Typical Uses	Court Approval Required
Cost recovery agreement	An agreement between the EPA and a PRP that addresses only the reimbursement of EPA costs. It takes the form of an administrative agreement.	Cost recovery. AOCs for work (1) may include a provision that requires the PRP to reimburse the EPA for past work costs and (2) will include a provision that requires the PRP to pay the EPA's future costs for overseeing the PRP's work. Such provisions are considered "cost recovery" because the costs are billed to the PRP after they are incurred by the EPA.	No
"Cash-out" agreement	Sometimes it is more appropriate for PRPs not to be involved in performing work at a site. In such cases, the EPA may negotiate a "cash-out" agreement with a PRP, under which the PRP pays an appropriate amount of estimated site costs before the work is done. Agreements to cash out de minimis PRPs take the form of AOCs, and agreements to cash out peripheral and other parties that have the ability to pay take the form of administrative agreements.	The EPA uses the money to help pay for the cleanup.	Yes, if a judicial CD

2.3   Corrective Action Process Under RCRA

The corrective action process under RCRA is similar to that under CERCLA. It generally consists of the following three steps:

1. *RCRA Facility Investigation (RFI)* — An RFI is similar to a CERCLA remedial investigation and includes the assessment of both active and inactive solid waste management units. The RFI identifies releases that require corrective action when contamination levels exceed action levels established under the state regulations.

2. *Corrective Measures Study (CMS)* — A CMS has an objective similar to that of an FS under CERCLA; it is intended to evaluate appropriate cleanup alternatives for eliminating or reducing the risks posed by releases discovered during the RFI.

3. *Corrective Measures Implementation (CMI)* — The CMI phase involves constructing and operating the remedy (or remedies) selected after completion of the CMS.

A company should contemplate each step when evaluating its environmental liabilities. As information becomes available during assessments, the company should continually reevaluate whether it is probable that subsequent corrective actions will be required and whether the costs of such actions are reasonably estimable.

2.4   Environmental Regulations — State

Both the EPA and state environmental agencies regulate the impact of business operations on the environment. The EPA develops and enforces regulations that implement environmental laws enacted by Congress. Similarly, state agencies develop and enforce regulations that implement laws enacted by a state's legislature. Further, under certain federal environmental laws, state regulatory agencies may earn authorization to promulgate regulations to implement and enforce a federal program if the state regulations are at least as stringent as the federal standards.

2.4.1   Federal-State Partnerships

The principle of cooperative federalism underlies the major environmental regulatory statutes enacted by Congress in the 1970s, including the CWA and RCRA. In such statutes, federal and state governments share some degree of regulatory authority. A federal law may allow states to assume responsibility for carrying out a regulatory program if the states demonstrate that they have adequate resources to implement and enforce the law. Federal authorization of a state program is usually a prerequisite for receiving federal funding to help support the program.

States are asked to implement and enforce federal laws while retaining the power to create laws that are more stringent than federal laws. Thus, the vast majority of federal environmental laws are implemented by states. The same is largely true for Indian tribes, which remain sovereign over their lands. In incorporating cooperative federalism principles into environmental laws, Congress has recognized the roles that states have historically played as protectors of their resources, as well as the local nature of many environmental issues.

Federal environmental laws that states help enforce include the following:

Clean Air Act — States have the primary responsibility to carry out the CAA through state implementation plans. The EPA approves state programs and must monitor the programs for continued compliance.

Clean Water Act — A state may be delegated with the authority to issue an NPDES permit if the state demonstrates, among other things, that it has adequate resources to address violations of the permit or the permit program through civil and criminal penalties and other ways and means of enforcement. The EPA retains enforcement authority under the CWA even when the NPDES permitting process has been delegated to a state.

Resource Conservation and Recovery Act — The EPA issues federal regulations under RCRA. States can establish their own waste statutes and regulatory schemes based on RCRA's requirements. If the EPA finds that these state regulatory efforts are consistent with the federal requirements, it will authorize state agencies to implement and enforce RCRA. State agency action to implement and enforce RCRA has the same force and effect as EPA action.

Surface Mining Control and Reclamation Act (SMCRA) — This act establishes a federal framework that, in the absence of state regulations, regulates mining activities. A state may avoid the federal requirements by establishing its own laws to substitute for the SMCRA's requirements.

In a federal-state partnership, state environmental regulations implement the federal environmental regulatory requirements. Further, in circumstances in which federal environmental statutes are silent about a state's responsibility to implement the requirements, states have developed and implemented environmental laws to protect local environmental resources. Most importantly, for companies managing environmental liabilities, each state has implemented environmental cleanup statutes and regulations to enforce the remediation of releases of hazardous substances into the environment. When the complexity and hazards of contamination do not rise to the level of the Superfund, which is regulated by the EPA, the states regulate the environmental cleanup activities at the local level.

2.4.2 State Environmental Cleanup Regulations

Many states have enacted pollution remediation laws that are similar to CERCLA and the remediation provisions of RCRA. State environmental laws and regulations, like federal environmental laws, may impose liability on (1) current owners and operators of a facility where hazardous substances were previously released or are in danger of being released and (2) entities that owned or operated the facility at the time the hazardous substances were disposed of at the facility (i.e., the historical owners and operators). The state environmental rules set standardized procedures for the assessment, monitoring, cleanup, reporting, and postresponse action care of properties under state jurisdiction.

Such procedures require an owner or operator to notify the state regulatory agency if contamination has been identified at concentrations that exceed specified "action levels" defined in the applicable rules. For example, under the Texas Risk Reduction Program (TRRP) regulated by the Texas Commission on Environmental Quality (TCEQ), when there is an actual or probable human exposure to a COC at a concentration that exceeds the Tier 1 human health protective concentration limit (the Texas "cleanup standard"), the regulated entity must notify the TCEQ of the contamination and then conduct response actions specified under TRRP. That is, even if the state regulatory agency has not initiated an enforcement action, the regulated entity has an obligation under the state environmental statute to notify the regulator and then conduct cleanup activities in compliance with the state environmental regulatory regime. Most state environmental regulations impose a similar notification provision to ensure that the regulator and any potentially affected parties (e.g., neighboring property owners) are properly notified.

Most of these regulations allow regulated entities to pursue environmental remediation activities under one of the following schemes:

- *Corrective action programs* — The state regulator uses a "command-and-control" method to lead remediation activities. Legal documents such as administrative orders may be used to direct the action, and the regulated entity must receive approval from the regulator at each step of the process. This process is similar to that for remediation activities regulated by the EPA under CERCLA and RCRA.

- *Voluntary cleanup/remediation programs* — The regulated entity (sometimes called the "volunteer") leads remediation activities and receives administrative, technical, and legal incentives from the state regulator to encourage cleanup of contaminated sites. State voluntary cleanup programs (VCPs) usually allow the entity to use risk-based cleanup principles, discussed below, in determining site-specific cleanup standards and remedial approaches.

Note that the term "voluntary" does not mean that the remediation activities are optional or discretionary. If a regulated entity does not proceed under the VCP, the state has the authority to direct the cleanup under a corrective action or similar program. Therefore, since a company's obligations under a state VCP are not undertaken voluntarily and at the sole discretion of management, they are considered to be environmental obligations and should be accounted for under the guidance in ASC 410-30.

2.4.2.1 Remedial Action Process

The remedial action process under state environmental regulations is similar to the federal CERCLA and RCRA processes. The table below identifies (1) the steps under CERCLA and RCRA, respectively, and (2) the state equivalents.

Process Step	CERCLA	RCRA	State Equivalents
1	RI	Facility investigation	RI, site investigation report, affected property assessment report
2	FS	CMS	FS, remedial alternatives analysis
3	Remedial action plan	CMS	Remedial action plan, remedial action work plan
4	ROD	Statement of basis	Remedial action plan, remedial action work plan
5	Remedial design	CMI	Remedial action plan, remedial action work plan
6	Remedial action	CMI	Remedial action
7	OM&M	CMI	Response action effectiveness report, monitoring reports

2.4.2.2 Permits

Some state environmental laws require companies to obtain a permit before they can (1) emit or discharge a pollutant into air or water, (2) dispose of hazardous waste, or (3) engage in certain regulated activities. Federal, state, and local government agencies also use permits to implement environmental laws intended to protect specific types of resources such as wetlands or endangered species. Most environmental permits are issued by state governments and may impose obligations related to long-term monitoring activities or facility closure activities.

RCRA permits are frequently issued by state agencies (and sometimes by EPA regional offices) to help ensure the safe treatment, storage, and disposal of hazardous waste. Like operational provisions, landfill permits issued under RCRA impose an ARO at the end of the life of the landfill. RCRA permits also impose obligations on owners and operators of RCRA hazardous waste management facilities to investigate and clean up on-site and off-site contamination caused by current and historic activities. Because many states are authorized by the EPA to operate state-led corrective action programs, these state-issued RCRA permits are regulatory drivers that companies must consider when determining their environmental obligations and AROs.

2.4.3 Transaction-Triggered Environmental Laws

During the early 1980s, commercial transactions became the target of state environmental laws that linked real estate deals to government-sanctioned and government-monitored environmental cleanups. These "transaction-triggered" (or transfer) statutes are intended to target and ensure the cleanup of hazardous substances at particular locations when specific events trigger application of the laws. For example, the New Jersey Industrial Site Recovery Act (ISRA) requires the owner or operator of an industrial establishment to investigate and remediate the property in anticipation of a property transfer, such as when the business ceases operations or is sold. As a precondition to the property transfer, the New Jersey Department of Environmental Protection (NJDEP) must issue a "no further action" (NFA) letter, approve a remedial action work plan, or execute a remediation agreement with the owner. ISRA is intended to ensure that a financially responsible party remains obligated to perform any necessary remediation after closing. It is also important to note that ISRA is triggered, and additional investigation and remediation may be required, even if the site is already subject to federal cleanup procedures under CERCLA or RCRA. Therefore, dual pathways for investigation and remediation may be ongoing to comply with this transfer statute.

States with transfer laws that similarly impose an obligation to perform assessment and remediation activities in connection with a transaction include, but may not be limited to, the following:

- *Connecticut* — The Connecticut Transfer Act applies to the transfer of (1) establishments at which hazardous waste is or was generated, (2) establishments to which hazardous waste was brought from a different location, and (3) certain defined business operations. The Transfer Act requires the transferor to notify both the transferee and the Connecticut Department of Energy and Environmental Protection at the time of transfer about whether a release of hazardous waste or substances has occurred at the establishment. If such a release has occurred, one of the parties to the transaction must commit to cleaning it up.

- *Delaware* — The Delaware Transfer or Closure of Establishments Law requires that, during the transfer of properties or operations, or the termination of operations at which at least one million pounds of hazardous substances are used or generated, environmental investigations be performed and financial assurances established to ensure that the site will be stabilized or secured.

Other states, such as California, Iowa, Michigan, and Oregon, do not specifically mandate environmental cleanup as a prerequisite to transactions but require disclosure of environmental conditions before the transfer of an interest in real property or a business. A seller with knowledge of an actual or suspected hazardous substance release must disclose to the buyer the general nature and extent of the release. Failure to comply with the disclosure requirements may impose civil and criminal liability, as well as harsh penalties such as strict liability for the cost to remediate the release.

2.4.4 Licensed Environmental Professionals

Several states have enacted laws establishing programs that license private environmental professionals to oversee the assessment and remediation of contaminated sites. Usually, a licensed environmental professional (LEP) is a member of the third-party environmental consulting firm conducting the assessment and remediation activities on behalf of the owner or operator. Under these programs, the role and responsibilities of the consultant have expanded from the responsibilities under the state-led programs. Some states, such as Connecticut, Massachusetts, and New Jersey, have these types of licensing programs.

In 1993, the Massachusetts Department of Environmental Protection (MassDEP) implemented new rules for reporting, assessing, and cleaning up releases of oil and hazardous material. Collectively known as the Massachusetts Contingency Plan (MCP), the rules lay out a detailed process for when and how contaminated sites must be assessed and cleaned up. The rules privatized the cleanup of contaminated sites in Massachusetts to allow the state to focus its limited resources on the tasks requiring government attention. Under the MCP, responsible parties are required to hire a licensed site professional (LSP) to manage and oversee the required assessment and cleanup activities. An LSP is an environmental scientist or engineer experienced in the cleanup of oil and hazardous material contamination. The LSP works with responsible parties to develop and execute a scope of work that will satisfy the state requirements set forth in the MCP for addressing contaminated property.

In 2009, New Jersey reformed its site remediation process to shift much of the responsibility for remediation oversight and approvals from the NJDEP to private contractors. These contractors must meet the state licensing requirements for certification as licensed site remediation professionals (LSRPs) and are required to comply with all remediation statutes and rules. They are bound by a strict code of ethics, violation of which could result in the assessment of penalties and suspension or revocation of an LSRP's license. In most situations, the NJDEP is not required or authorized to (1) review and approve investigation and cleanup plans in advance or (2) issue NFA letters at the conclusion of cleanup activities. Rather, the LSRPs determine the propriety of the work at the conclusion of the investigations and cleanups and issue the final sign-off document, known as the "response action outcome" (RAO). An LSRP issues an RAO only after a site has been properly investigated and remediated in accordance with the remediation standards and technical requirements for site remediation. The NJDEP monitors the LSRP's remediation progress and actions by requiring that forms and reports be submitted as remediation milestones are reached.

In Connecticut, LEPs are authorized to work on sites that qualify as "establishments" if a transfer of ownership is involved. Under the Connecticut Transfer Act, an establishment is any facility where dry cleaning, furniture stripping, or auto body repairs have been conducted; any facility where hazardous waste has been treated, stored, recycled, handled, or disposed of; or any other facility where more than 100 kilograms of hazardous waste has been generated in any one month. LEPs may also investigate and remediate contaminated sites under the voluntary remediation program and verify that a parcel has complied with remediation standard regulations.

As a result of licensing programs, the time required to complete remediation activities has decreased in the states noted above. Before the licensing programs were established, cleanups at some sites took more than 20 years to complete because of delays associated with state agency review and approval turnaround times. Now that the LEP is the decision maker, cleanups in most cases are driven by the real estate market and are performed in less time than the period allowed by statute. All three states report that the rate of site closure exceeds the rate of discovery and that case backlogs have therefore decreased.

2.4.5 Risk-Based Cleanup

Like many responsible parties, state environmental agencies are seeking methods that will allow the use of available monetary resources to accomplish the greatest reduction in risk. Most state environmental agencies have adopted a risk-based decision-making process to provide a framework for determining cleanup requirements at contaminated sites. Risk-based programs aim to protect human health and the environment while providing more options for fulfilling regulatory requirements associated with remediation of contaminated properties. Under these risk-based programs, owners and operators can most often achieve regulatory closure more cost-effectively, and return the affected property to productive use more quickly.

The basic premise of risk-based remediation is that the decision to remediate a site should be based on the need to reduce the actual or potential risk that specific contaminants pose to human or ecological receptors. Risk-based decision-making involves (1) the evaluation of current and reasonably likely future risks to human health and the environment associated with contamination at a site and (2) use of that information to develop the best combination of cleanup and site management to reduce risks to acceptable levels. The process includes identification of hazards, assessment of exposure and toxicity, characterization of risk, and informed decision-making. Fully informed decisions about potential remedial actions cannot be made without adequate site characterization to identify the nature and extent of contamination. This information is gathered during site assessment processes and presented in a conceptual site model or similar assessment report.

As noted in Section 2.2.4.2.5, for a risk to exist, there must be (1) a source of chemical release, (2) a human or ecological receptor that is potentially exposed to the released chemicals, and (3) an environmental exposure pathway connecting the source and the receptor(s). The chart below lists examples of these elements.

Sources of Chemical Release	<ul><li>Surface spills.</li><li>Historical releases from industrial plants and storage containers.</li><li>Leaking landfills.</li><li>Leaking aboveground or underground storage tanks and tank appurtenances.</li></ul>
Receptors of Chemical Release	Human:<ul><li>Dermal contact with soil, sediment, or contaminated water outdoors.</li><li>Ingestion of soil, sediment, or contaminated water.</li><li>Ingestion of food sources (e.g., plants, aquatic species) that contain bioaccumulated chemicals from contaminated water, air, or soil.</li><li>Inhalation of indoor air or air in a confined space.</li></ul>Ecological:<ul><li>Ecosystems (e.g., wetlands, rivers).</li><li>Animals and other living species (e.g., endangered or protected species, fish, or birds).</li></ul>
Transport Pathways	<ul><li>Migration of chemicals within subsurface soil.</li><li>Leaching to groundwater and surface water (desorption from soil and sediment).</li><li>Groundwater to surface water (and vice versa).</li><li>Volatilization from soil or groundwater to indoor air.</li><li>Erosion and surface water runoff.</li></ul>

If any of these elements is absent, the exposure pathways are incomplete and no risk is present. If a risk *is* present, it may be reduced or eliminated through (1) removal of the source or receptor or (2) interruption of the pathway. The goal of risk-based remediation is to reduce present and future risk in a cost-effective manner through the use of one or more of the following risk reduction techniques:

- *Chemical source reduction* — Achieved by physical removal or control of the COCs.

- *Receptor restriction* — Land use controls (e.g., restrictive covenants) and physical barriers (e.g., concrete caps and site fencing) can prevent COC exposure until source concentrations are reduced below risk levels.

- *Chemical pathway elimination* — Examples include placing restrictions on excavation or groundwater use to prevent on-site or off-site receptors from making contact with chemicals of concern.

Risk-based cleanup standards provide greater flexibility because they are based on actual land use (e.g., commercial or industrial) rather than unrealistic maximum exposure assumptions (e.g., pristine conditions). If future land use can be controlled and groundwater use can be restricted, less stringent cleanup standards can be applied because risk is mitigated. Risk-based cleanup standards allow flexibility to choose between a more rapid and costly remediation approach, which may provide more immediate, unrestricted land use, or a less expensive natural attention option, which would most likely require long-term monitoring and restrictions on both land and groundwater use.

2.5 Environmental Regulations — International

Most developed and many developing countries have enacted remediation laws, some of which are more far-reaching than CERCLA and RCRA. In addition, international environmental law has evolved to address the interdependence of ecosystems that traverse political boundaries. For environmental law in the world of sovereign states, the challenge is to reconcile the fundamental independence of each state with the inherent interdependence of ecosystems. Accordingly, the role of nonstate actors and international organizations has expanded. For example, in 2004, the European Union enacted a broad directive aimed at preventing environmental damage by requiring industrial polluters to pay prevention and remediation costs. In addition, the Basel Convention on the Control of Transboundary Movements of Hazardous Wastes and Their Disposal is the most comprehensive global environmental agreement on hazardous and other wastes and has 183 member parties. Levels of enforcement of environmental laws vary widely among different countries.

In Latin America, as a result of rapid industrialization, population growth, increased economic power, and complex environmental and natural resource challenges, environmental law has evolved to stronger laws, greater enforcement, and increased liability. For example, because of pressure from local citizen groups and nongovernmental organizations to address environmental challenges, enforcement of environmental laws in Latin America is trending upward. The enforcement efforts are often high profile, widely reported in the news media, and intended to set examples through high penalty assessments and criminal convictions.

Chapter 3 — Accounting for Environmental Obligations

The primary objective of ASC 410-30 is to provide accounting guidance on environmental remediation liabilities arising from pollution or contamination caused by some past act or event. The recognition guidance in ASC 410-30 is generally based on the framework outlined in ASC 450-20, which requires the recognition of a loss when (1) it is probable that a loss has been incurred and (2) the amount of the loss can be reasonably estimated. However, ASC 410-30 provides incremental and interpretive guidance on how to apply these recognition criteria specifically to environmental obligations in the context of the legal framework established in the United States. That is, while ASC 450-20 broadly addresses the accounting for all loss contingencies, ASC 410-30 provides additional guidance on accounting for a subset of loss contingencies (specifically, environmental remediation liabilities), as illustrated below.

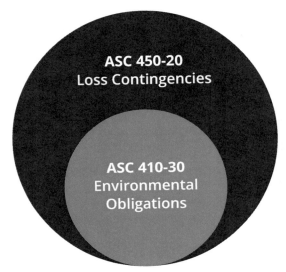

ASC 410-30 provides guidance on measuring an estimated environmental remediation liability, including which costs to include in the estimate, how to consider the effects of future developments, and how to allocate the liability among PRPs. In addition, ASC 410-30 addresses the accounting for potential recoveries of environmental losses from insurance providers or other third parties. However, as discussed in Chapter 2, CERCLA imposes a liability scheme that differs from traditional common law and statutory liability schemes. Specifically, a liability under CERCLA is joint and several; therefore, each PRP is potentially liable for the entire cost of cleanup. This liability scheme poses challenges to the application of ASC 410-30 when measuring a PRP's allocable share of an environmental remediation liability once the recognition criteria have been met.

Several years can elapse from the time a reporting entity is named as a PRP to when the environmental remediation process is completed. Because of the amount of time required to remediate a site, the complexity of the legal framework, and the number of parties that may be responsible for paying the costs related to a site, it can be difficult to determine when to recognize and how to measure an environmental remediation liability.

The remainder of this chapter provides an in-depth discussion of the recognition and measurement guidance in ASC 410-30, as well as examples that illustrate how the concepts discussed are commonly applied in practice.

3.1 Scope of ASC 410-30

ASC 410-30

Entities

15-1 The provisions of this Subtopic apply to all entities. This Subtopic provides guidance on accounting for environmental remediation liabilities and is written in the context of operations taking place in the United States; however, the accounting guidance is applicable to all the operations of the reporting entity.

15-2 The recognition and measurement guidance in this Subtopic should be applied on a site-by-site basis.

Transactions

15-3 The guidance in this Subtopic does not apply to the following transactions and activities:

    a. Environmental contamination incurred in the normal operation of a long-lived asset (see Subtopic 410-20 for guidance that will apply if the entity is legally obligated to treat the contamination). Paragraph 410-20-15-3(b) explains that the obligation to clean up the spillage resulting from the normal operation of the fuel storage facility is within the scope of Subtopic 410-20. Additionally, that Subtopic applies if a legal obligation to treat environmental contamination is incurred or assumed as a result of the acquisition, construction, or development of a long-lived asset.

    b. Pollution control costs with respect to current operations or on accounting for costs of future site restoration or closure that are required upon the cessation of operations or sale of facilities, as such current and future costs and obligations represent a class of accounting issues different from environmental remediation liabilities.

    c. Environmental remediation actions that are undertaken at the sole discretion of management and that are not induced by the threat, by governments or other parties, of litigation or of assertion of a claim or an assessment.

    d. Recognizing liabilities of insurance entities for unpaid claims.

    e. Natural resource damages and toxic torts (see paragraphs 450-20-55-10 through 55-21).

    f. Asset impairment issues.

While ASC 410-30 is written specifically in the context of U.S. environmental laws, the Codification excerpt above specifies that the subtopic applies to all entities that comply with U.S. GAAP regardless of location. In addition, the excerpt clarifies that the "unit of account" for recognizing and measuring environmental remediation liabilities is the individual site. Therefore, a reporting entity with foreign operations must understand the relevant laws and regulations governing environmental remediation obligations in the foreign jurisdictions in which it operates so that it can properly apply the guidance in ASC 410-30. Further, with respect to environmental remediation obligations in the United States, a reporting entity must also consider state laws and regulations, if applicable.

Connecting the Dots

As noted in ASC 410-30-15-3(c), the guidance in ASC 410-30 does not apply to "[e]nvironmental remediation actions that are undertaken at the sole discretion of management and that are not induced by the threat . . . of litigation or of assertion of a claim or an assessment." Therefore, ASC 410-30 does not require the recognition of a liability for environmental remediation activities voluntarily undertaken by a reporting entity. The decision to incur the costs of performing such environmental remediation activities in the future does not give rise to a present liability since the entity has considerable discretion in changing its plans and avoiding the expenditure. The determination of whether an environmental remediation action is voluntary or induced by the threat of litigation involves considerable judgment and should be based on all relevant facts and circumstances.

3.2 Recognition of Environmental Remediation Liabilities

Environmental remediation liabilities arise when a reporting entity is (or was) associated with a particular site at which remedial actions must take place. The recognition guidance in ASC 410-30-25-3 is generally consistent with CERCLA's recognition of various types of PRPs, which is discussed in Section 2.2.7. As illustrated in the diagram below, ASC 410-30-25-3 acknowledges six types of involvement that a reporting entity may have with a site.

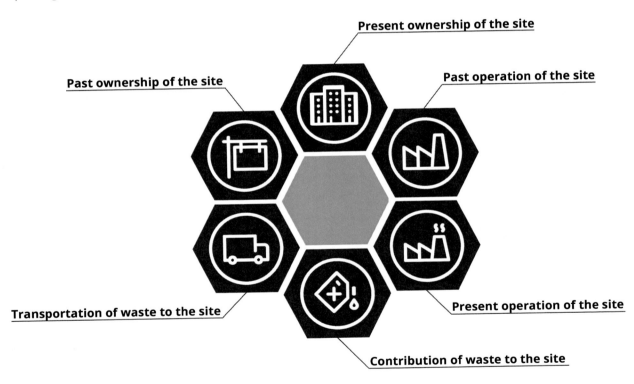

For an environmental remediation liability to be recognized in the financial statements, one of the types of involvement illustrated above must have occurred before the reporting date. Once this condition is met, recognition of an environmental obligation is based on the framework in ASC 450-20, which requires a reporting entity to recognize a liability if (1) it is probable that a loss has been incurred and (2) the amount of that loss can be reasonably estimated.

In addition to the general recognition framework in ASC 450-20, there are several recognition benchmarks in ASC 410-30 that correlate with the various stages of the environmental remediation process that the EPA generally applies. Under ASC 410-30, a reporting entity is required, at a minimum, to evaluate whether it needs to recognize an environmental remediation liability upon the occurrence of each of the benchmarks. Further, ASC 410-30 mandates the recognition of a liability upon the occurrence of certain benchmarks. However, the benchmarks in ASC 410-30 are not meant to override the general recognition criteria outlined in ASC 450-20. The diagram below illustrates the relationship between the recognition framework in ASC 450-20 and the recognition benchmarks in ASC 410-30.

**A reporting entity is required to recognize an
environmental remediation liability upon the earlier of:**

Meeting recognition criteria under ASC 450-20	The occurrence of certain benchmarks under ASC 410-30

Sections 3.2.1 and 3.2.2 below focus on the application of (1) the recognition framework in ASC 450-20 to environmental remediation liabilities and (2) the specific recognition benchmarks included in ASC 410-30.

3.2.1 Probability That a Liability Has Been Incurred (the "Probability Criterion")

ASC 410-30

25-4 In the context of environmental remediation liabilities, the probability criterion in paragraph 450-20-25-2 consists of two elements; the criterion is met if both of the following elements are met on or before the date the financial statements are issued or are available to be issued (as discussed in Section 855-10-25):

   a. Litigation has commenced or a claim or an assessment has been asserted, or, based on available information, commencement of litigation or assertion of a claim or an assessment is probable. In other words, it has been asserted (or it is probable that it will be asserted) that the entity is responsible for participating in a remediation process because of a past event.

   b. Based on available information, it is probable that the outcome of such litigation, claim, or assessment will be unfavorable. In other words, an entity will be held responsible for participating in a remediation process because of the past event.

25-5 What constitutes commencement or probable commencement of litigation or assertion or probable assertion of a claim or an assessment in relation to particular environmental laws and regulations may require legal determination.

25-6 Given the legal framework within which most environmental remediation liabilities arise, there is a presumption that the outcome of such litigation, claim, or assessment will be unfavorable if both of the following conditions exist:

   a. Litigation has commenced or a claim or an assessment has been asserted, or commencement of litigation or assertion of a claim or assessment is probable.

   b. The reporting entity is associated with the site — that is, it in fact arranged for the disposal of hazardous substances found at a site or transported hazardous substances to the site or is the current or previous owner or operator of the site.

Generally, the determination of whether it is probable that a liability has been incurred (i.e., whether the probability criterion is met) is a factual matter. That is, if an environmental site has been identified for remediation and available evidence connects a reporting entity with that site, the probability criterion is generally met. This evidence can be discovered internally (e.g., through environmental studies) or externally (e.g., upon notification from the EPA).

Connecting the Dots

We believe that the probability criterion is met once an entity has received a general or special notice letter from the EPA identifying the entity as a PRP (see Section 2.2.7). Such notification represents the assertion of a claim or assessment, as well as evidence that an entity is associated with the site.

However, that is not to say that an entity must receive a notice letter from the EPA to conclude that the probability criterion has been met. Rather, an entity is required to evaluate (1) whether pollution or contamination has occurred at a particular site as a result of the entity's current or prior involvement with the site and (2) whether it is probable that remediation will be required for that site. Therefore, a conclusion that it is probable that a liability has been incurred may be reached before the entity receives a notice letter from the EPA identifying it as a PRP.

The example below illustrates the application of the probability criterion.

Example 3-1

Operator X is aware of contamination at Site A resulting from the release of hazardous substances for which X had arranged disposal. While federal and state environmental regulations hold X liable for the remediation of Site A, no actions have been taken against X. No studies related to Site A have been prepared, and X does not plan to commence remediation actions until the regulators force it to do so. However, X believes that if the regulators were aware of the contamination, it is probable that they would force X to clean up Site A.

In this scenario, we believe that the probability criterion has been met because (1) X is legally liable for the cleanup and (2) X believes that it is probable that the regulators would assert a claim or assessment against X and thereby force X to clean up Site A if they were aware of the contamination. Since X was directly involved in arranging for the disposal of hazardous substances at Site A and it is probable that the regulators would assert a claim or assessment against X, there is a presumption that the outcome of such a claim or assessment would be unfavorable, and the probability criterion has been met (see ASC 410-30-25-6).

The following flowchart summarizes the FASB's guidance on determining whether the probability criterion has been met:

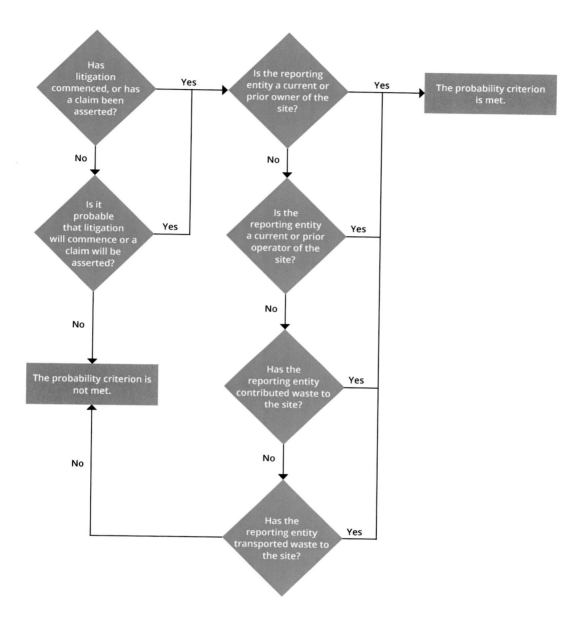

3.2.2 Ability to Reasonably Estimate the Liability (the "Estimable Criterion")

ASC 410-30

25-7 Estimating environmental remediation liabilities involves an array of issues at any point in time. In the early stages of the process, cost estimates can be difficult to derive because of uncertainties about a variety of factors. For this reason, estimates developed in the early stages of remediation can vary significantly; in many cases, early estimates later require significant revision. The following are some of the factors that are integral to developing cost estimates:

a. The extent and types of hazardous substances at a site

b. The range of technologies that can be used for remediation

c. Evolving standards of what constitutes acceptable remediation

d. The number and financial condition of other potentially responsible parties and the extent of their responsibility for the remediation (that is, the extent and types of hazardous substances they contributed to the site).

25-8 Section 450-20-55 concludes that the criterion for recognition of a loss contingency in paragraph 450-20-25-2(b) is met when a range of loss can be reasonably estimated.

25-9 An estimate of the range of an environmental remediation liability typically is derived by combining estimates of various components of the liability (such as the costs of performing particular tasks, or amounts allocable to other potentially responsible parties but that will not be paid by those other potentially responsible parties), which are themselves likely to be ranges. For some of those component ranges, there may be amounts that appear to be better estimates than any other amount within the range; for other component ranges, there may be no such best estimates. Accordingly, the overall liability that is recorded may be based on amounts representing the lower end of a range of costs for some components of the liability and best estimates within ranges of costs of other components of the liability.

25-10 At the early stages of the remediation process, particular components of the overall liability may not be reasonably estimable. This fact should not preclude the recognition of a liability. Rather, the components of the liability that can be reasonably estimated should be viewed as a surrogate for the minimum in the range of the overall liability.

25-11 For example, a sole potentially responsible party that has confirmed that it sent waste to a Superfund site and agrees to perform a remedial investigation and feasibility study may know that it will incur costs related to the remedial investigation-feasibility study. The potentially responsible party, although aware that the total costs associated with the site will be greater than the cost of the remedial investigation-feasibility study, may be unable to reasonably estimate the overall liability because of existing uncertainties, for example, regarding the kinds and quantities of hazardous substances present at the site and the technologies available to remediate the site. This lack of ability to quantify the total costs of the remediation effort, however, shall not preclude recognition of the estimated cost of the remedial investigation-feasibility study. In this circumstance, a liability for the best estimate (or, if no best estimate is available, the minimum amount in the range) of the cost of the remedial investigation-feasibility study and for any other component remediation costs that can be reasonably estimated shall be recognized in the entity's financial statements.

25-12 Uncertainties relating to the entity's share of an environmental remediation liability shall not preclude the entity from recognizing its best estimate of its share of the liability or, if no best estimate can be made, the minimum estimate of its share of the liability, if the liability is probable and the total remediation liability associated with the site is reasonably estimable within a range (see paragraphs 410-30-30-1 through 30-7).

25-13 Uncertainties are pervasive in the measurement of environmental remediation liabilities, and reporting entities are required to recognize their best estimate at the particular point in time (or, if no best estimate can be made, the minimum estimate) of their share of the liability and to refine their estimate as events in the remediation process occur.

The recognition guidance in ASC 410-30-25-7 through 25-13 acknowledges that it is often difficult to estimate the total cost of environmental remediation, particularly in the early stages of the remediation process (e.g., when a reporting entity is named a PRP). However, such difficulty during the estimation process does not automatically preclude recognition of a liability. Rather, a reporting entity must attempt to estimate the cost of the environmental remediation upon determining that the probability criterion is met.

Generally, a point estimate of the total cost to remediate an environmental site will not be determinable in the early stages of the remediation process given the number of external factors typically involved in site cleanup. Rather, total cost will become estimable over time as more information becomes available as a result of performing the required remediation steps. However, ASC 410-30-25-9 acknowledges that "an environmental remediation liability typically is derived by combining estimates of various components of the liability." For example, the components of the total liability may consist of (1) completion of a remedial investigation, (2) completion of an FS, (3) remedial design, (4) the remediation itself, and (5) postremediation monitoring. ASC 410-30-25-11 states that if any one component of the environmental remediation liability is reasonably estimable, that estimate should be used as the minimum in the range of total costs to remediate the site. Therefore, we generally believe that an entity will be able to reasonably estimate the environmental remediation liability (i.e., the estimable criterion will be met) in the early stages of the cleanup process on the basis of the costs of completing a particular component of the liability, which the entity can use to establish a minimum amount.

We have observed that reporting entities sometimes delay the recognition of an environmental remediation liability because of certain misconceptions about meeting the estimable criterion. The diagram below illustrates some common misconceptions, along with our interpretive responses to these misconceptions.

Misconception About Meeting the Estimable Criterion	Interpretive Response
A liability should not be recognized if the total cost of the entire remediation effort is not reasonably estimable.	Often, it will not be possible to estimate the total cost of the entire environmental remediation process. In such a case, ASC 410-30 requires a reporting entity to evaluate the individual components of the environmental remediation process to determine whether it can reasonably estimate one or more of the components. Accordingly, the reporting entity would be required to recognize a liability for each component that can be reasonably estimated even if the total cost of site remediation cannot be reasonably estimated.
A liability should not be recognized if a reporting entity's allocable share of an environmental remediation obligation (when the entity is one of several PRPs) is uncertain.	If the total liability, or a component of the liability, can be reasonably estimated, the reporting entity should estimate its allocable share (or a range of allocable shares) in accordance with the guidance in ASC 410-30-30-5 and 30-6. Environmental remediation liabilities are typically joint and several. Therefore, a reporting entity may be financially responsible for the entire remediation effort even if it contributed very little to the overall contamination of the site.
If more than one course of action has been proposed (i.e., there are multiple remediation alternatives), a liability should not be recognized until a specific course of action has been selected.	We generally believe that when an FS or other proposed course of action contains several remediation alternatives, a range of the total remediation costs has been established. If one course of action is more likely to be taken than the others, that course of action should be used for recognizing the liability. Conversely, if each course of action is equally likely to be taken, the alternative with the lowest cost estimate establishes the low end of the range and should be used for recognizing the liability. However, if one of the alternatives is "no action" and has a cost estimate of zero, the entity should disregard that alternative when establishing the range. The "no action" alternative simply provides a baseline for comparison with other alternatives and therefore does not represent a viable alternative with respect to remediating a site (see Section 3.3.1.2).

The example below illustrates the application of the estimable criterion.

Example 3-2

Company Z receives notification from the EPA that it is a PRP at Site B because of its role as a transporter of waste to the site. Therefore, Z concludes that the probability criterion has been met.

Company Z is one of many entities identified as PRPs at Site B, and as of the date Z receives the notice from the EPA, no site study has been initiated or prepared. Upon receiving notice from the EPA, Z concludes that the cost of performing the entire remediation effort at Site B is not reasonably estimable. However, on the basis of Z's prior experience with similar environmental remediation obligations, Z estimates that the cost of the RI/FS will range from $5 million to $15 million. Further, given Z's previous work at similar sites and its role in the contamination at Site B, Z expects to be responsible for only 2 percent to 5 percent of the total cleanup costs at Site B. Therefore, Z determines that a range of costs is reasonably estimable for a *component* of the overall cleanup effort.

In addition, Z concludes that no single amount or percentage appears to be a better estimate than any other amount or percentage in the range. Therefore, Z measures its liability by using the low end of the range and records a liability of $100,000 ($5 million × 2%).

3.2.3 Recognition Benchmarks

Sections 3.2.1 and 3.2.2 describe the overall recognition framework prescribed by ASC 410-30. However, ASC 410-30 also lists specific benchmarks that an entity must consider when evaluating (1) the probability that a loss has been incurred and (2) the extent to which any loss related to an environmental obligation is reasonably estimable.

ASC 410-30

25-14 Certain stages of a remediation effort or process and of potentially responsible party involvement (see paragraphs 410-30-05-24 for a discussion of these stages) provide benchmarks that should be considered when evaluating the probability that a loss has been incurred and the extent to which any loss is reasonably estimable. Benchmarks should not, however, be applied in a manner that would delay recognition beyond the point at which the recognition criteria in Subtopic 450-20 are met.

25-15 The following are recognition benchmarks for a Superfund remediation liability; analogous stages of the Resource Conservation and Recovery Act corrective-action process are also indicated. At a minimum, the estimate of a Superfund (or Resource Conservation and Recovery Act) remediation liability should be evaluated as each of these benchmarks occurs.

a. Identification and verification of an entity as a potentially responsible party. The Resource Conservation and Recovery Act analogue is subjection to facility permit requirements. Receipt of notification or otherwise becoming aware that an entity may be a potentially responsible party compels the entity to action. The entity must examine its records to determine whether it is associated with the site. If, based on a review and evaluation of its records and all other available information, the entity determines that it is associated with the site, it is probable that a liability has been incurred. If all or a portion of the liability is reasonably estimable, the liability shall be recognized. In some cases, an entity will be able to reasonably estimate a range of its liability very early in the process because the site situation is common or similar to situations at other sites with which the entity has been associated (for example, the remediation involves only the removal of underground storage tanks in accordance with the underground storage tank program). In such cases, the criteria for recognition would be met and the liability shall be recognized. In other cases, however, the entity may have insufficient information to reasonably estimate the minimum amount in the range of its liability. In these cases, the criteria for recognition would not be met at this time.

ASC 410-30 (continued)

b. Receipt of unilateral administrative order. The Resource Conservation and Recovery Act analogue is, generally, interim corrective measures. An entity may receive a unilateral administrative order compelling it to take a response action at a site or risk penalties of up to four times the cost of the response action. Such response actions may be relatively limited actions, such as the performance of a remedial investigation and feasibility study or performance of a removal action, or they may be broad actions such as remediating a site. Under section 106 of Superfund, the Environmental Protection Agency must find that an "imminent and substantial endangerment" exists at the site before such an order may be issued. No preenforcement review by a court is authorized under Superfund if an entity elects to challenge a unilateral administrative order. The ability to estimate costs resulting from unilateral administrative orders varies with factors such as site complexity and the nature and extent of the work to be performed. The benchmarks that follow should be considered in evaluating the ability to estimate such costs insofar as the actions required by the unilateral administrative order involve these benchmarks. The cost of performing the requisite work generally is estimable within a range, and recognition of an environmental remediation liability for costs of removal actions generally should not be delayed beyond this point.

c. Participation, as a potentially responsible party, in the remedial investigation-feasibility study. The Resource Conservation and Recovery Act analogue is Resource Conservation and Recovery Act facility investigation. At this stage, the entity and possibly others have been identified as potentially responsible parties and have agreed to pay the costs of a study that will investigate the extent of the environmental impact of the release or threatened release of hazardous substances and identify site-remediation alternatives. Further, the total cost of the remedial investigation-feasibility study generally is estimable within a reasonable range. In addition, the identification of other potentially responsible parties and their agreement to participate in funding the remedial investigation-feasibility study typically provides a reasonable basis for determining the entity's allocable share of the cost of the remedial investigation-feasibility study. At this stage, additional information may be available regarding the extent of environmental impact and possible remediation alternatives. This additional information, however, may or may not be sufficient to provide a basis for reasonable estimation of the total remediation liability. At a minimum, the entity should recognize its share of the estimated total cost of the remedial investigation-feasibility study. As the remedial investigation-feasibility study proceeds, the entity's estimate of its share of the total cost of the remedial investigation-feasibility study can be refined. Further, additional information may become available based on which the entity can refine its estimates of other components of the liability or begin to estimate other components. For example, an entity may be able to estimate the extent of environmental impact at a site and to identify existing alternative remediation technologies. An entity may also be able to identify better the extent of its involvement at the site relative to other potentially responsible parties; the universe of potentially responsible parties may be identified; negotiations among potentially responsible parties and with federal and state Environmental Protection Agency representatives may occur; and information may be obtained that materially affects the agreed-upon method of remediation.

d. Completion of feasibility study. The Resource Conservation and Recovery Act analogue is corrective measures study. At substantial completion of the feasibility study, both a minimum remediation liability and the entity's allocated share generally will be reasonably estimable. The feasibility study should be considered substantially complete no later than the point at which the potentially responsible parties recommend a proposed course of action to the Environmental Protection Agency. If the entity had not previously concluded that it could reasonably estimate the remediation liability (the best estimate or, if no amount within an estimated range of loss was a better estimate than any other amount in the range, the minimum amount in the range), recognition should not be delayed beyond this point, even if uncertainties, for example, about allocations to individual potentially responsible parties and potential recoveries from third parties, remain.

e. Issuance of record of decision. The Resource Conservation and Recovery Act analogue is approval of corrective measures study. At this point, the Environmental Protection Agency has issued its determination specifying a preferred remedy. Normally, the entity and other potentially responsible parties have begun, or perhaps completed, negotiations, litigation (see paragraphs 410-30-35-8 through 35-11), or both for their allocated share of the remediation liability. Accordingly, the entity's estimate normally can be refined based on the specified preferred remedy and a preliminary allocation of the total remediation costs.

ASC 410-30 (continued)

f. Remedial design through operation and maintenance, including postremediation monitoring. The Resource Conservation and Recovery Act analogue is corrective measures implementation. During the design phase of the remediation, engineers develop a better sense of the work to be done and are able to provide more precise estimates of the total remediation cost. Further information likely will become available at various points until the site is delisted, subject only to postremediation monitoring. The entity should continue to refine and recognize its best estimate of its final obligation as this additional information becomes available.

The diagram below illustrates the relationship between the recognition benchmarks outlined above and the probability and reasonably estimable criteria discussed in ASC 410-30-25-4 through 25-13.

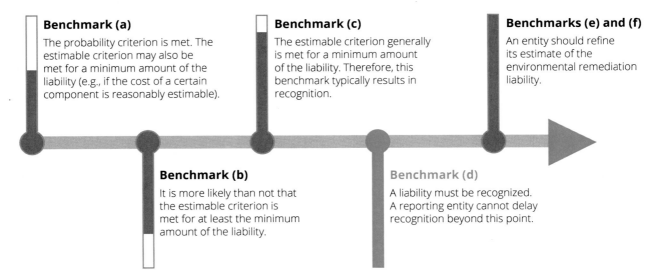

Benchmark (a)

The probability criterion is met. The estimable criterion may also be met for a minimum amount of the liability (e.g., if the cost of a certain component is reasonably estimable).

Benchmark (c)

The estimable criterion generally is met for a minimum amount of the liability. Therefore, this benchmark typically results in recognition.

Benchmarks (e) and (f)

An entity should refine its estimate of the environmental remediation liability.

Benchmark (b)

It is more likely than not that the estimable criterion is met for at least the minimum amount of the liability.

Benchmark (d)

A liability must be recognized. A reporting entity cannot delay recognition beyond this point.

Connecting the Dots

As noted above, recognition benchmark (d) in ASC 410-30-25-15 states that an environmental remediation liability must be recognized upon "substantial completion of [a] feasibility study." Benchmark (d) further states that an FS is "substantially complete no later than the point at which the potentially responsible parties recommend a proposed course of action to the [EPA]." Therefore, benchmark (d) inherently presumes that the FS will always be completed and issued by the PRPs.

We have observed in practice that the EPA is not legally required to follow the steps in the order described in ASC 410-30 and that therefore, these recognition benchmarks do not always occur in sequential order. Consequently, it is possible that the EPA will perform and complete its own FS for an environmental site. An EPA-conducted FS may be performed in lieu of, or in addition to, a PRP-conducted FS. Thus, a PRP-recommended course of action, as referenced in benchmark (d), may not always take place, or it may occur after the EPA's completion of an FS and related recommended course of action.

We believe that regardless of whether an FS and a proposed course of action are completed by the PRPs or by the governmental agency charged with making the ultimate remediation decision, they provide the type of evidence necessary for a reporting entity to make a reliable estimate and therefore require recognition of an environmental remedial liability in a manner consistent with ASC 410-30-25-15(d). Thus, we believe that if the EPA completes an FS for a particular site before the PRPs have recommended their proposed course of action, benchmark (d) is met and a liability must be recognized at the time the EPA completes the FS.

The example below illustrates the application of the recognition benchmarks.

Example 3-3

Company C has been identified as one of many PRPs at a Superfund site. All of the PRPs formed a group (the "PRP Group") to (1) coordinate efforts with the EPA and (2) allocate the costs of completing the environmental remediation. Given the scope of the remediation, the EPA and the PRP Group performed separate RIs/FSs. Company C has agreed to fund 15 percent of the total cost of the PRP Group's RI/FS.

On November 22, 20X6, the EPA published its RI/FS. As of this date, the PRP Group had not yet completed its RI/FS. The EPA's RI/FS contains four alternative proposed courses of action for remediating the Superfund site but does not specify the EPA's preferred remedy. Cost estimates for the site remediation range from $500 million to $1.5 billion. Before the release of the EPA's RI/FS, C recognized a liability for its allocable share of the cost of completing the PRP Group's RI/FS. However, C did not record an environmental remediation liability for the remediation and postremediation components of the cleanup effort.

Recognition benchmark (d) was met on November 22, 20X6, even though the PRP Group had not substantially completed its RI/FS. Therefore, C should recognize an additional liability for its allocable share of the estimated cost of remediating the Superfund site. The additional liability should be based on C's best estimate of its share of the remediation liability or, if no best estimate can be made, C's minimum estimate of its allocable share of the total remediation liability.

3.2.4 Capitalization of Environmental Costs

While environmental costs are generally charged to expense as incurred, they may be capitalized in certain circumstances, as noted below.

ASC 410-30

25-18 Those costs may be capitalized if recoverable but only if any one of the following criteria is met:

a. The costs extend the life, increase the capacity, or improve the safety or efficiency of property owned by the entity. For purposes of this criterion, the condition of that property after the costs are incurred must be improved as compared with the condition of that property when originally constructed or acquired, if later.

b. The costs mitigate or prevent environmental contamination that has yet to occur and that otherwise may result from future operations or activities. In addition, the costs improve the property compared with its condition when constructed or acquired, if later.

c. The costs are incurred in preparing for sale that property currently held for sale.

The examples in the implementation guidance of ASC 410-30-55, some of which are reproduced below, elaborate on the application of criteria (a) and (b) in ASC 410-30-25-18, which require that the costs incurred result in a future economic benefit.

ASC 410-30

Example 5: Illustrations of Whether Costs to Treat Environmental Contamination Should Be Capitalized or Charged to Expense

Case D: Lead Pipes in Office Building That Contaminate Drinking Water

55-22 The following table provides a summary for determining whether costs to treat environmental contamination should be capitalized or charged to expense.

Environmental Contamination, Treatments	Evaluation of Criteria
Lead Pipes in Office Building Contaminate Drinking Water: A. Remove lead pipes and replace with copper pipes	1. Removing the lead pipes has improved the safety of the building's water system compared with its condition when the water system was built or acquired. 2. By removing the lead pipes, the building's owner eliminated an existing environmental problem and prevented any further contamination from that lead. However, by removing the existing pipes, the building's owner has not mitigated or prevented environmental problems yet to occur, if any, from future operation of the building. Conclusion: Costs to remove the lead pipes and install copper pipes may be capitalized under the first criterion. The book value of the lead pipes should be charged to expense when removed.

Case E: Soil Contamination Caused by an Operating Garbage Dump

55-23 The following table provides a summary for determining whether costs to treat environmental contamination should be capitalized or charged to expense.

Environmental Contamination, Treatments	Evaluation of Criteria
Soil Contamination Caused by an Operating Garbage Dump: A. Refine soil on dump property	1. The life of a garbage dump is not extended by refining its soil. Further, the condition of the soil after refining will not be improved over its condition when the garbage dump was constructed or acquired. Removal of the toxic waste restores the soil to its original uncontaminated condition. 2. Removal of toxic waste from the soil addresses an existing environmental concern. It also prevents that waste from leaching in the future. However, removing the waste does not mitigate or prevent future operations from creating future toxic waste. The risk will continue regardless of how much of the existing soil is refined. Conclusion: Soil refinement costs should be charged to expense unless the garbage dump is currently held for sale and the costs were incurred to prepare the garbage dump for sale.

ASC 410-30 (continued)

(Table continued)

Environmental Contamination, Treatments	Evaluation of Criteria
B. Install liner	1. The liner does not extend the useful life or improve the efficiency or capacity of the garbage dump. However, the liner has improved the garbage dump's safety compared to when the dump was constructed or acquired.
	2. The liner addresses an existing and potential future problem. In this example, the garbage dump contains toxic waste from past operations and will likely generate toxic waste during future operations. The liner partly addresses the existing environmental problem by preventing future leaching of existing toxic waste into the soil. The liner also mitigates or prevents leaching of toxic waste that may result from garbage dumping in future periods and has improved the garbage dump's safety compared to when the dump was constructed or acquired.
	Conclusion: The liner may be capitalized under either the first or second criterion.

Case F: Water Well Contamination

55-24 The following table provides a summary for determining whether costs to treat environmental contamination should be capitalized or charged to expense.

Environmental Contamination, Treatments	Evaluation of Criteria
Water Well Contamination Caused by Chemicals That Leaked Into Wells Containing Water That Will Be Used in Future Beer Production:	
A. Neutralize water in wells	1. The treatment does not extend the life of the wells, increase their capacity, or improve efficiency. The condition of the water is not safer after the treatment compared to when the wells were initially acquired.
	2. By neutralizing the water, the possibility of future contamination of the wells from future operations has not been mitigated or prevented.
	Conclusion: Costs incurred to neutralize well water should be charged to expense unless the wells were held for sale and the costs were incurred to prepare the wells for sale.
B. Install water filters	1. The water filters improve the safety of the wells compared with their uncontaminated state when built or acquired.
	2. The water filters address future problems that may result from future operations. Since the water filters are effective in filtering environmental contamination, they mitigate the effect of spilling new contaminants into the wells during future operations. In addition, the water filters represent an improvement compared with the wells' original condition without water filters.
	Conclusion: The water filtering system may be capitalized under either the first or the second criterion.

ASC 410-30 (continued)

Case G: Underground Gasoline Storage Tank Leak

55-25 The following table provides a summary for determining whether costs to treat environmental contamination should be capitalized or charged to expense.

Environmental Contamination, Treatments	Evaluation of Criteria
Underground Gasoline Storage Tanks Leak and Contaminate the Company's Property:	
A. Refine soil	1. Soil refinement does not extend the useful life, increase the capacity, or improve the efficiency or safety of the land relative to its unpolluted state when acquired.
	2. By refining the contaminated soil, the oil company has addressed an existing problem. However, the company has not mitigated or prevented future leaks during future operations.
	Conclusion: Soil refining costs should be charged to expense unless the property is currently held for sale and the costs were incurred to prepare the property for sale.
B. Encase tanks so as to prevent future leaks from contaminating surrounding soil	1. In some cases, encasement may increase the life of the tanks because of their increased resistance to corrosion, leaking, etc. In other situations, the treatment may not increase the life of the tanks. However, the encasement has improved the tanks' safety compared with their condition when built or acquired.
	2. Encasement has mitigated or prevented future leakage and soil contamination that might otherwise result from future operations. In addition, the encasement has improved the tanks' safety compared with their condition when built or acquired.
	Conclusion: The cost of encasement may be capitalized under either the first or the second criterion.

Case H: Air in Office Building Contaminated With Asbestos Fibers

55-26 The following table provides a summary for determining whether costs to treat environmental contamination should be capitalized or charged to expense.

Environmental Contamination, Treatments	Evaluation of Criteria
Air in Office Building Contaminated With Asbestos Fibers:	
A. Remove asbestos	1. Removal of the asbestos improves the building's safety over its original condition since the environmental contamination (asbestos) existed when the building was constructed or acquired.
	2. By removing the asbestos, the building's owner has eliminated an existing problem and has prevented any further contamination from that asbestos. However, by removing the existing asbestos, the building's owner has not mitigated or prevented new environmental problems, if any, that might result from future operation of the building.
	Conclusion: Asbestos removal costs may be capitalized as a betterment under the first criterion.

Conversely, there is limited guidance illustrating the application of criterion (c) in ASC 410-30-25-18, which requires that the "costs are incurred in preparing for sale that property currently held for sale." We believe that the premise of this criterion is that the environmental costs provide a probable future economic benefit to the reporting entity in the form of improved salability (to the extent that such costs are recoverable).

When determining whether environmental costs associated with property held for sale can be capitalized, an entity must identify the timing of recognition and underlying cause of the costs incurred. For example, the entity would first assess whether the recognition criteria for an environmental remediation liability were met before the property was classified as held for sale. It would generally be inappropriate to capitalize environmental costs while the property is held for sale if such costs should have been recognized before the property was held for sale.

Similarly, costs associated with legal obligations to remediate property would typically not be incurred in "preparing for sale" since such obligations would exist regardless of whether the property is sold. This concept is supported by the example in ASC 410-30-55-21, which states, in part:

> Fines paid in connection with violations of the Clean Air Act should be charged to expense. Even if the plant is currently held for sale, the fines should be charged to expense because the costs would not have been incurred to prepare the plant for sale.

Therefore, we believe that the following types of costs would typically qualify for capitalization under ASC 410-30-25-18(c):

- Costs that the reporting entity voluntarily incurred to improve the salability of an asset.

- Costs incurred at the request of a buyer that would otherwise not be a liability of the reporting entity.

The examples below illustrate the differences between environmental remediation costs that are capitalizable (Example 3-4) and those that are not capitalizable (Example 3-5).

Example 3-4

Company A has property held for sale. To improve the salability of the property, A incurs costs to remediate environmental concerns that it is not legally obligated to address.

In this scenario, the costs are incurred voluntarily and are directly associated with preparing the property for sale (i.e., the costs would be avoided if the property were not for sale). Therefore, the remediation costs incurred may qualify for capitalization under ASC 410-30-25-18(c), subject to the held-for-sale measurement guidance in ASC 360-10-35-43.

Example 3-5

Company A has property held for sale. The due diligence efforts of a prospective buyer reveal land contamination associated with an accidental chemical spill that occurred in a prior period. Because site contamination has been identified, A is legally obligated under local environmental law to perform remediation activities.

In this scenario, ASC 410-30-25-18(c) is not applicable even though an ASC 410-30 environmental obligation is initially identified while the property is classified as held for sale. While the prospective buyer may require A to perform remediation work related to the identified environmental obligation, the obligation in itself is unrelated to the preparation for sale. That is, remediation is required because of a legal obligation that (1) will be settled irrespective of a potential transfer of the property to a new owner and (2) may have qualified for recognition before the property was held for sale.

> **Example 3-5 (continued)**
>
> Alternatively, if the prospective buyer required A to address certain environmental matters as a condition to closing on the sale and A was not under a preexisting ASC 410-30 legal obligation to address those matters, an agreement with the prospective buyer to perform certain remediation activities may be within the scope of ASC 410-30-25-18(c).

3.3 Initial Measurement of Environmental Remediation Liabilities

Once a reporting entity has determined that it is probable that an environmental remediation liability has been incurred, the entity should estimate the liability on the basis of available information. As illustrated below, the initial measurement guidance in ASC 410-30 involves a two-step process.

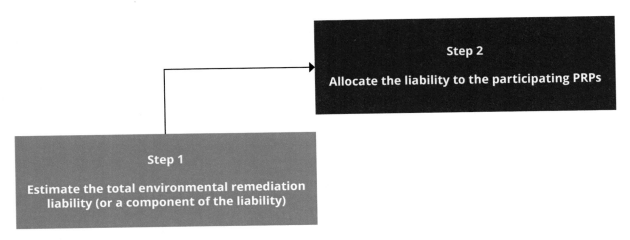

3.3.1 Estimating Environmental Remediation Costs

The first step in the measurement of an environmental remediation liability is to develop an estimate of the total cost of completing a remediation effort. The estimation process should include each site for which a reporting entity has concluded that the recognition criteria have been met (i.e., estimates should be prepared on a site-by-site basis). If the total cost of completing the entire remediation effort is not reasonably estimable, the reporting entity should develop its estimate for the individual components of the remediation process that *are* reasonably estimable. For example, at the onset of the remediation effort, the reporting entity may not be able to estimate the total cost of completing the entire remediation effort; however, it may be able to estimate the cost of performing the RI/FS.

Regardless of whether the reporting entity develops a cost estimate for completing the entire remediation effort or just a component, the estimate should encompass the *total* cost of completing such effort or component thereof (i.e., the cost that will ultimately be allocated to all PRPs, as opposed to only the reporting entity's estimated allocable portion of the cost). As discussed in Section 3.3.2, the reporting entity would then record its allocable share of the environmental remediation liability.

Estimating the costs of completing the total environmental remediation effort or a component thereof involves significant judgment and depends on key assumptions, including:

- The types of costs that should be included in the measurement of the liability.

- The remediation method that is expected to be approved to complete the remediation effort.

- The effects of expected future events and developments.

These assumptions are discussed below.

3.3.1.1 Types of Costs to Be Included in the Measurement of an Environmental Remediation Liability

ASC 410-30

30-10 Costs to be included in the measurement are the following:

a. Incremental direct costs of the remediation effort (see paragraph 410-30-55-1)

b. Costs of compensation and benefits for those employees who are expected to devote a significant amount of time directly to the remediation effort, to the extent of the time expected to be spent directly on the remediation effort.

30-11 The remediation effort is considered on a site-by-site basis; it includes the following:

a. Precleanup activities, such as the performance of a remedial investigation, risk assessment, or feasibility study and the preparation of a remedial action plan and remedial designs for a Superfund site, or the performance of a Resource Conservation and Recovery Act of 1976 facility assessment, facility investigation, or corrective measures studies

b. Performance of remedial actions under Superfund, corrective actions under the Resource Conservation and Recovery Act of 1976, and analogous actions under state and non-U.S. laws

c. Government oversight and enforcement-related activities

d. Operation and maintenance of the remedy, including required postremediation monitoring.

30-12 Determining any of the following is part of the remediation effort:

a. The extent of remedial actions that are required

b. The type of remedial actions to be used

c. The allocation of costs among potentially responsible parties.

The costs of making such determinations, including legal costs, shall be included in the measurement of the remediation liability.

30-13 The costs of services related to routine environmental compliance matters and litigation costs involved with potential recoveries are not part of the remediation effort.

30-14 Litigation costs involved with potential recoveries shall be charged to expense as incurred until realization of the claim for recovery is considered probable and an asset relating to the recovery is recognized, at which time any remaining such legal costs shall be considered in the measurement of the recovery.

30-15 The determination of what legal costs are for potential recoveries rather than for determining the allocation of costs among potentially responsible parties will depend on the specific facts and circumstances of each situation. For purposes of measuring environmental remediation liabilities, the measurement shall be based on enacted laws and adopted regulations and policies. No changes should be anticipated. The remedial action plan that is used to develop the estimate of the liability shall be based on the methodology that is expected to be approved to complete the remediation effort.

30-16 Costs to defend against assertions of liability in the context of environmental remediation liabilities involve determining whether an entity is responsible for participating in a remediation process.

ASC 410-30 (continued)

30-17 The measurement of environmental remediation liabilities shall be based on the reporting entity's estimate of what it will cost to perform each of the elements of the remediation effort (determined in accordance with paragraphs 410-30-30-11 through 30-15) when those elements are expected to be performed. Although this approach is sometimes referred to as considering inflation, it does not simply rely on an inflation index (cost estimates submitted to the Environmental Protection Agency usually include a prescribed inflation factor) and should take into account factors such as productivity improvements due to learning from experience with similar sites and similar remedial action plans. In situations in which it is not practicable to estimate inflation and such other factors because of uncertainty about the timing of expenditures, a current-cost estimate would be the minimum in the range of the liability to be recorded until such time as these cost effects can be reasonably estimated.

30-18 When an overall liability is estimated by combining estimates of various components of the liability, additional possible losses present in the component estimates must be considered in determining an overall additional possible loss.

The table below summarizes the types of costs that are included in and excluded from the measurement of an environmental remediation liability in accordance with ASC 410-30-30-13, ASC 410-30-30-17, and ASC 410-30-55-1 through 55-3.

Types of Costs	Included	Excluded
Legal costs related to:		
Determining the extent of remedial actions that are required	✓	
Determining the type of remedial actions to be used	✓	
Determining the allocation of costs among PRPs	✓	
Potential recoveries		⊘
Routine environmental compliance matters		⊘
Costs related to completing an RI/FS	✓	
Fees to outside engineering and consulting firms for site investigations and the development of remedial action plans and remedial designs	✓	
Fees to contractors for performing remedial actions	✓	
Governmental oversight costs and past costs (e.g., costs incurred by the EPA or any other governmental authority dealing with a site)	✓	
The cost of machinery and equipment that are dedicated to the remedial actions and do not have an alternative use	✓	
Assessments by a PRP group covering costs incurred by the group in dealing with a site	✓	
Costs of operation and maintenance of the remedial action, including the costs of postremediation monitoring required by the remedial action plan	✓	
Costs of compensation and benefits for employees who are expected to devote a significant amount of time directly to the remediation effort (to the extent of the time expected to be spent directly on the remediation effort)	✓	

(Table continued)

Types of Costs	Included	Excluded
The following costs, to the extent that such items can be reasonably estimated:		
Inflation	✓	
Productivity improvements (as a result of learning from experience with similar sites or remediation actions)	✓	

As discussed in Section 2.2.6, the EPA may sometimes require PRPs to indefinitely perform OM&M for remedies that contain wastes on-site or include institutional controls. Accordingly, questions have arisen about how a PRP should estimate the costs of OM&M when the period over which such activities will be performed is indefinite. We have observed that while it is common practice for entities to accrue OM&M costs over a 30-year period on a rolling basis, there is no basis under U.S. GAAP for arbitrarily truncating the forecasting period. Instead, the reporting entity should develop its best estimate of what it will cost to perform OM&M for the site (which may be a range).

Further, while legal costs related to potential recoveries are specifically excluded from the measurement of an environmental remediation liability, we believe that estimated costs that an entity expects to incur to defend itself against assertions of liability related to an environmental site may be included in the measurement of an environmental remediation liability as an accounting policy election that should be consistently applied. The EITF Agenda Committee discussed a similar issue with respect to accruing future legal costs for loss contingencies but did not reach a recommendation for the Task Force. ASC 450-20-S99-2 includes the following related to this issue:

> The Task Force discussed a potential new issue relating to the accounting for legal costs expected to be incurred in connection with a FASB Statement No. 5, *Accounting for Contingencies* [codified as ASC 450-20], loss contingency. Some Task Force members observed that they believe practice typically has expensed such costs as incurred; however, other Task Force members suggested that practice may not be consistent in this area. The Task Force declined to add this potential new issue to its agenda.

> The SEC Observer noted that the SEC staff would expect a registrant's accounting policy to be applied consistently and that APB Opinion No. 22, *Disclosure of Accounting Policies* [codified as ASC 235], requires disclosure of material accounting policies and the methods of applying those policies.

In the absence of further guidance from the FASB or the SEC staff, entities should apply the SEC staff guidance noted at the EITF Agenda Committee meeting referenced above, which requires disclosure and consistent application of an entity's accounting policy.

3.3.1.2 Remediation Method That Is Expected to Be Approved

ASC 410-30-30-15 states, in part:

> The remedial action plan that is used to develop the estimate of the liability shall be based on the methodology that is expected to be approved to complete the remediation effort.

Further, ASC 410-30-35-5 states:

> Once a methodology has been approved, that methodology and the technology available shall be the basis for estimating the liability until it is probable that there will be formal acceptance of a revised methodology.

As discussed in Chapter 2, the interested parties (i.e., the EPA and PRPs) will often consider several alternative remediation methods when determining the best course of action for remediating a particular environmental site. The choice of an alternative method is generally affected by (1) the nature, location, and volume of contaminants; (2) the number of different toxins; (3) the existing remediation standards; and (4) the disruption to wildlife or the local community. For example, remediation alternatives may take into account the effects of different options for removing contaminants from the site (e.g., on-site or off-site disposal) or the advantages and disadvantages of targeting specific key areas ("hotspots") of the site rather than conducting a complete remediation (i.e., bank-to-bank dredging). Each alternative is typically accompanied by cost estimates, which can vary significantly. Ultimately, the EPA will consider the cost estimates of each alternative method when determining which method to approve. However, making this determination can be very time-consuming because the EPA considers input from a number of affected constituents, such as local community members and advocacy groups, as well as from other regulatory departments, if applicable.

While there may be uncertainty about which method will ultimately be approved, we believe that a range of remediation costs is established once cost estimates for the various remediation alternatives have been developed. Therefore, the reporting entity would need to measure its environmental remediation liability by using either the most likely point within the range or, if no single point estimate is better than the others, the minimum amount within the range.

Connecting the Dots

In developing cost estimates for alternative remediation methods, the EPA commonly includes a "no action" alternative, which is generally represented by a cost estimate of zero. While this could be interpreted to mean that the range of cost estimates starts with zero as the low end of the range, the "no action" alternative is included for the sole purpose of providing a baseline for comparison with other alternatives and is not provided as a viable alternative with respect to remediating an environmental site. Therefore, when an entity evaluates the low end of a range of costs of possible remediation alternatives, we do not believe that the "no action" alternative should be considered as part of the range.

In addition, as described in Section 3.2.3, it is possible that both the EPA and a PRP group will conduct an FS for a particular site. In such situations, the EPA and PRP group may (1) consider different remediation alternatives or (2) develop different cost estimates for the same remediation alternative. In those instances, the various alternatives and cost estimates prepared by the EPA and the PRP group would establish a range. The reporting entity would then be required to measure its environmental remediation liability by using the most likely point within the range of cost estimates developed by the EPA and PRP group or, if no single point estimate within the range provides an estimate that is better than the others, the minimum amount within the range.

Connecting the Dots

When the EPA conducts its own FS at a site, it commonly specifies its "preferred remedy" among the alternative remediation methods it considered. Historically, the ultimate record of decision (ROD) issued by the EPA in such situations has generally been consistent with the preferred remedy specified in the FS. Therefore, we believe that there is a rebuttable presumption that the preferred remedy specified in an EPA-conducted FS represents the "methodology that is expected to be approved to complete the remediation effort," as contemplated in ASC 410-30-30-15. Thus, if a reporting entity does not demonstrate sufficient evidence to overcome the rebuttable presumption, the entity should develop its cost estimates by using the EPA's preferred remedy "until it is probable that there will be formal acceptance of a revised methodology," as noted in ASC 410-30-35-5.

However, there may be instances in which a PRP group has developed cost estimates for the preferred remedy that differ from those published by the EPA. Accordingly, it is possible that two sets of cost estimates will exist for the same remediation method (i.e., the EPA's cost estimates and the PRP group's cost estimates). In our experience, the cost estimates included in the ROD issued by the EPA are generally not less than those that were included in the EPA's preferred remedy. Therefore, we generally believe that there is strong evidence that the environmental remediation liability measured on the basis of the cost estimates developed by the EPA for the EPA's preferred remedy represents the best estimate within the range of possible outcomes.

In accordance with the recognition guidance in ASC 410-30-25, the use of cost estimates associated with a remediation method other than the preferred remedy to measure an environmental remediation liability would require a determination that the other remediation methods and associated cost estimates provide either a better estimate or an equally good estimate.

During the remediation process, additional contaminants are sometimes discovered. Upon such an occurrence, different remediation methods and a longer remediation period may be necessary, ultimately increasing the total remediation cost. In situations in which additional contaminants are discovered, the environmental remediation liability must be adjusted as a change in accounting estimate and accounted for in accordance with ASC 250-10-45-17 through 45-20. See also Section 3.4.1.

3.3.2 Allocating Environmental Remediation Costs to Other PRPs

When more than one PRP has been identified for a particular site, the total costs associated with remediating the site may be allocated among the various PRPs. In this instance, ASC 410-30-30-1 specifies that the amount recorded by a reporting entity should be its allocable share of the total environmental remediation liability (or a component of the environmental remediation liability). However, when an environmental remediation liability is joint and several, each PRP may be held responsible for the entire cost of the remediation effort regardless of the amount of waste the PRP actually contributed to the site. Therefore, estimating the reporting entity's allocable share of a joint and several liability requires significant judgment, particularly in the early stages of remediation. However, uncertainty about a reporting entity's share of a joint and several liability does not preclude recognition.

Generally, a reporting entity's allocable share is a function of (1) its ability to negotiate allocation percentages with the other PRPs and (2) the ability of the other PRPs to pay their allocable share. We believe that the following three-step process should be used for estimating a reporting entity's allocable share of an environmental obligation:

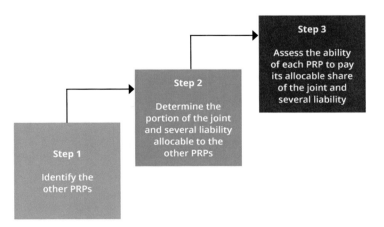

As a result of the three-step process, the reporting entity's allocable share of a joint and several liability is equal to (1) the total joint and several environmental remediation liability, less the amount allocable to other PRPs, plus (2) the reporting entity's share of any amounts that other PRPs are unable to pay.

3.3.2.1 Step 1 — Identify the Other PRPs

Generally, the EPA or other governmental authority overseeing the remediation of the environmental site performs this step. See Section 2.2.1 for a discussion of how the EPA identifies PRPs.

3.3.2.2 Step 2 — Determine the Portion of the Joint and Several Liability Allocable to the Other PRPs

To make this determination, the reporting entity must first classify the population of PRPs into the following categories, as defined in ASC 410-30-20:

- *Participating PRP* — "A party to a Superfund site that has acknowledged potential involvement with respect to the site. Active [PRPs] may participate in the various administrative, negotiation, monitoring, and remediation activities related to the site. Others may adopt a passive stance and simply monitor the activities and decisions of the more involved [PRPs]. This passive stance could result from a variety of factors such as the entity's lack of experience, limited internal resources, or relative involvement at a site. This category of potentially responsible parties (both active and passive) is also referred to as players."

- *Recalcitrant PRP* — "A party whose liability with respect to a Superfund site is substantiated by evidence, but that refuses to acknowledge potential involvement with respect to the site. Recalcitrant [PRPs] adopt a recalcitrant attitude toward the entire remediation effort even though evidence exists that points to their involvement at a site. Some may adopt this attitude out of ignorance of the law; others may do so in the hope that they will be considered a nuisance and therefore ignored. Typically, parties in this category must be sued in order to collect their allocable share of the remediation liability; however, it may be that it is not economical to bring such suits because the parties' assets are limited. This category of [PRPs] is also referred to as nonparticipating [PRPs]."

- *Unproven PRP* — "A party that has been identified as a [PRP] for a Superfund site by the [EPA] or by an analogous state agency, but that does not acknowledge potential involvement with respect to the site because no evidence has been presented linking the party to the site. Also referred to as a hiding-in-the-weeds [PRP]."

- *Unknown PRP* — "A party that has liability with respect to a Superfund site, but that has not yet been identified as a [PRP] by the [EPA] or by an analogous state agency."

- *Orphan share PRP* — "An identified [PRP] that cannot be located or that is insolvent. Some of these parties may be identified by the [EPA]; others may be identified as the site is investigated or as the remediation is performed. However, no contributions will ever be made by these parties."

ASC 410-30-30-4 establishes a rebuttable presumption that the joint and several liability should be allocated to only participating PRPs. That is, no portion of the liability should be allocated to the other four types of PRPs described above. Thus, the classification of PRPs can significantly affect the determination of the reporting entity's allocable share and, therefore, the amount recorded as an environmental remediation liability.

The example below illustrates the determination of a PRP's classification as a participating PRP.

Example 3-6

In 20X6, 100 companies, including Transport Co., were named PRPs at a Superfund site. The PRP group was held responsible for the remediation of a five-mile section of an Oregon river that had been contaminated by hazardous waste.

In 20X7, the PRP group entered into an allocation agreement to fund the cost of completing an RI/FS. Under the agreement, Transport Co. and PRPs 2 through 99 each received an allocation percentage of 0.5 percent, while PRP 100 received an allocation percentage of 50.5 percent. The allocation percentages were based on an initial study of the quantity and types of hazardous waste contributed by each PRP.

In 20X9, the EPA issued an AOC requesting the PRP group's participation in a time-critical removal action to address an imminent human health hazard identified at a specific location on the river. Transport Co. and PRPs 2 through 99 signed the AOC. However, PRP 100 disagreed with its allocable share of cleanup costs for the specified section of the river; therefore, it declined to execute the AOC and withdrew from the PRP group under protest, subject to a reservation of rights.

The EPA then issued a unilateral administrative order (UAO) requiring PRP 100 to perform removal-response activities related to the identified section of the river. Upon receiving notice of the UAO, PRP 100 notified both the PRP group and the EPA of its intention to comply with the UAO. PRP 100 continues to consult with the EPA on how it can comply with the UAO.

In this scenario, we believe that it is appropriate for Transport Co. to classify PRP 100 as a participating PRP (as opposed to a recalcitrant or other type of PRP) when estimating PRP 100's allocable share of the environmental remediation costs. This conclusion is based on the following factors:

- PRP 100 was a member of the PRP group from 20X7 to 20X9 and agreed to fund a portion of the costs of the 20X7 RI/FS during its membership in the group.
- Despite its withdrawal from the PRP group as a result of a disagreement over its allocable share of cleanup costs, PRP 100 subsequently agreed to comply with the EPA's UAO.

As more information becomes available during the remediation process, PRPs may "move" from one PRP category to another. For example, as the EPA learns more about the contamination at a site, it may identify additional PRPs. Such identification may result in the reclassification of certain entities from unknown PRPs to participating PRPs. Further, if a participating PRP subsequently becomes insolvent or otherwise unable to pay its allocable share because its financial condition changes, the PRP may move to the orphan share category. The reporting entity should update its assessment of which PRPs it considers participating (and, therefore, update its estimate of its allocable share) on the basis of the facts and circumstances in existence as of the financial statement issuance date.

While there are numerous ways to allocate a joint and several liability, allocation of environmental liabilities is generally based on one or more of the following factors, as described in ASC 410-30-55-4:

ASC 410-30

55-4 There are numerous ways to allocate liabilities among potentially responsible parties. The four principal factors considered in a typical allocation process are the following:

    a. Elements of fair share. Examples are the amount of waste based on volume; the amount of waste based on mass, type of waste, toxicity of waste; the length of time the site was used.

    b. Classification of potentially responsible party. Examples are site owner, site operator, transporter of waste, generator of waste.

    c. Limitations on payments. This characteristic includes any statutory or regulatory limitations on contributions that may be applicable to a potentially responsible party. For example, in the reauthorization of the Comprehensive Environmental Response, Compensation, and Liability Act, it has been proposed that the statute limit the contribution of a municipality to 10 percent of the total remediation liability, irrespective of the municipality's allocable share.

    d. Degree of care. This refers to the degree of care exercised in selecting the site or in selecting a transporter.

As noted in ASC 410-30-55-5, PRPs may agree among themselves to certain allocation percentages on the basis of one or more of the above factors, or they may engage an external consultant to perform the allocation. In addition, although we would expect PRPs to make this request only in rare circumstances, they may ask the EPA to assign allocation percentages, which are generally nonbinding.

ASC 410-30-30-5 states that the primary sources of evidence for the reporting entity's estimate of its allocable share of the joint and several liability are the allocation method and percentages that (1) the PRPs have agreed to (regardless of whether the PRPs' agreement applies to the entire remediation effort or to the costs incurred in the current phase of the remediation process), (2) have been assigned by a consultant, or (3) have been determined by the EPA. However, this guidance also states that the reporting entity should estimate its allocable share on the basis of "the allocation method and percentage that ultimately will be used for the entire remediation effort." Therefore, in certain situations, the allocation method and percentage resulting from one of the primary sources discussed above may differ from the allocation method and percentage that the reporting entity expects will ultimately be used to allocate the cost of the remediation effort. Under ASC 410-30-30-6, "[i]f the entity's estimate of the ultimate allocation method and percentage differs significantly from the method or percentage from these primary sources, the entity's estimate should be based on objective, verifiable information." ASC 410-30-30-6 provides the following examples of such objective, verifiable information:

- "Existing data about the kinds and quantities of waste at the site."

- "Experience with allocation approaches in comparable situations."

- "Reports of environmental specialists (internal or external)."

- "Internal data refuting [EPA] allegations about the entity's contribution of waste (kind, volume, and so forth) to the site."

Connecting the Dots

A PRP group will often agree to certain allocation percentages at an early stage of the remediation effort (e.g., at the RI stage), before each party's share of the ultimate remediation effort is known. Since the costs associated with an early stage are generally insignificant in relation to the total site remediation cost, the PRPs may agree to these percentages as a practical matter to comply with EPA requirements even if the percentages are not expected to reflect each PRP's ultimate share of the entire remediation effort. For example, before completing an RI, the PRP group may not have enough information to determine which contaminants each PRP contributed. Therefore, the PRPs may each agree to fund equal shares of the cost of completing the RI even if they do not expect to equally fund the entire site remediation cost.

As discussed above, ASC 410-30-30-5 states that the allocation percentages agreed to by the PRPs for the cost of the RI are a primary source of evidence for determining the reporting entity's allocable share. Accordingly, a conflict may arise between the overall objective of determining the reporting entity's allocable share based on the method and percentage "that ultimately will be used for the entire remediation effort" and the method and percentage that the PRP group agreed to for the current phase of such remediation effort (i.e., a primary source of evidence).

We generally believe that the percentages agreed on by the PRP group represent a primary source of evidence as described in ASC 410-30-30-5 and therefore serve as data points for estimating the reporting entity's allocable share of the total environmental remediation liability. Consequently, if the cost of the entire remediation effort becomes reasonably estimable before the PRP group has agreed to updated allocation methods or percentages, the reporting entity should generally consider allocation percentages that were previously agreed on when determining its allocable share of the additional environmental remediation liability since, in accordance with ASC 410-30-30-5(a), these allocation methods or percentages were agreed on for a phase of the remediation process. If the reporting entity believes that a different allocation method and percentage should be used, it should apply the guidance in ASC 410-30-30-6, which (1) indicates that the estimate "should be based on objective, verifiable information" and (2) provides examples of such information.

3.3.2.3 Step 3 — Assess the Ability of Each PRP to Pay Its Allocable Share of the Joint and Several Liability

After determining the portion of the environmental remediation liability that is allocable to the other PRPs, the reporting entity must assess the likelihood that they will pay that amount. This assessment involves significant judgment and is often difficult to perform. As part of the assessment, the reporting entity should learn about the financial condition of the other participating PRPs as of each reporting period. If the reporting entity determines that a participating PRP will not be able to pay its allocable share, the reporting entity's share of that PRP's allocable amount should be included in the measurement of the reporting entity's liability.

Example 3-7

Operator Co. has been identified as one of 10 parties potentially responsible for remediation of a Superfund site. The PRPs enter into an allocation agreement immediately before commencing the remediation effort. At this point, Operator Co. concludes that because the other PRPs are included in the allocation agreement, they are considered participating PRPs. Operator Co. also determines that the PRPs each have the financial wherewithal to fund their respective allocable shares of the remediation cost. Under the allocation agreement, Operator Co. and the other PRPs agree to the following allocation percentages:

Operator Co.	5%
PRPs 2–9	80% (10% each)
PRP 10	15%

However, Operator Co. is concerned about PRP 10's ability to pay its allocable share on the basis of unfavorable operating results in recent periods. Thus, Operator Co. decides to monitor PRP 10's quarterly filings so that it can determine whether its initial conclusion that PRP 10 was a participating PRP is still appropriate. Two years into the remediation process, PRP 10 files for bankruptcy as a result of its continued financial decline. Accordingly, Operator Co. determines that PRP 10 should be reclassified as an orphan share PRP. Thus, Operator Co. updates its estimate of its allocation percentage by calculating its allocable portion of PRP 10's share as follows:

Orphan share	15.0%
Operator Co.'s pro rata share of the orphan share	5.9%*
Amount of orphan share allocated to Operating Co.	0.9%**
Operator Co.'s initial allocation percentage	5.0%
Operator Co.'s revised allocation percentage	5.9%

*   Operator Co. calculates its pro rata share of the orphan share by dividing its initial allocation percentage (5 percent) by the initial aggregate percentage allocated to PRPs 2 through 9 and itself (85 percent).

**   The amount of the orphan share that is allocated to Operator Co. is equal to the orphan share of 15 percent multiplied by Operator Co.'s allocable share of the orphan share of 5.9 percent, as calculated in the footnote above.

3.4 Subsequent Measurement of Environmental Remediation Liabilities

3.4.1 Changes in Estimates

Determining the amount of an environmental remediation liability depends on a wide range of variables that constantly change as new information becomes available. Circumstances that may result in changes to the recorded amount of an environmental remediation liability include the following:

- Changes in a reporting entity's allocable share of the liability because of:
  - The EPA's identification of additional PRPs.
  - Movement of PRPs between categories (e.g., from recalcitrant to participating or vice versa).
  - The ability of other PRPs to pay their full allocable share.
  - Different allocation percentages agreed to by the PRPs (or assigned by a consultant or the EPA).

- Additional phases of the remediation process that become reasonably estimable as progress is made.

- Changes in underlying cost estimates for completion of each phase of the cleanup (e.g., the cost of compensation and employee benefits).

- Changes in laws and regulations.

- Changes in the method approved by the EPA.

- Changes in technology used for applying the approved method.

Since the estimated costs of remediation change on the basis of new information, they are considered changes in estimates under ASC 250 and should be recognized in the period in which they occur.

3.4.2 Consideration of Future Events

ASC 410-30

35-2 Additional complexities arise if other potentially responsible parties are involved in an identified site. The costs associated with remediation of a site ultimately will be assigned and allocated among the various potentially responsible parties. The final allocation of costs may not be known, however, until the remediation effort is substantially complete, and it may or may not be based on an entity's relative direct responsibility at a site. An entity's final obligation depends, among other things, on the willingness of the entity and other potentially responsible parties to negotiate a cost allocation, the results of the entity's negotiation efforts, and the ability of other potentially responsible parties associated with the particular site to fund the remediation effort.

35-3 The time period necessary to remediate a particular site may extend several years, and the laws governing the remediation process and the technology available to complete the remedial action may change before the remedial action is complete. Additionally, the impact of inflation and productivity improvements can change the estimates of costs to be incurred.

35-4 The impact of changes in laws, regulations, and policies shall be recognized when such changes are enacted or adopted.

The typical environmental remediation process spans many years because of the complexity associated with treating the site and monitoring it on a go-forward basis. During this time, environmental laws may change and, as a result, affect the estimated cost of the remediation effort. ASC 410-30 indicates that the measurement of an environmental remediation liability should be based on currently enacted laws and adopted regulations and policies (i.e., future changes in environmental laws should not be anticipated).

In addition, the technology that is used to remediate an environmental site constantly changes throughout the life cycle of the cleanup effort. Changes in available technology often result in lower-than-expected costs to clean up the site. However, ASC 410-30-35-5 states that "[o]nce a methodology has been approved, that methodology **and the technology available** shall be the basis for estimating the liability until it is probable that there will be formal acceptance of a revised methodology" (emphasis added). Therefore, when measuring an environmental remediation liability, a reporting entity should consider only the technology that is currently available to perform the actions required for the approved remediation method. If and when it becomes probable that a revised method will be approved, the reporting entity should update its cost estimate on the basis of the technology that is currently available for applying that revised method.

3.4.3   Discounting Environmental Liabilities

ASC 410-30-35-12 indicates that reporting entities are permitted, but not required, to discount environmental liabilities if both of the following criteria are met:

- The "aggregate amount of the liability or component" is "fixed or reliably determinable."

- The "amount and timing of cash payments for the liability or component are fixed or reliably determinable."

With respect to the determination of whether both criteria are met, ASC 410-30-35-12 defines the "amount of the liability or component" as "the reporting entity's allocable share of the undiscounted joint and several liability." The guidance also clarifies that the "unit of account" for assessing whether the criteria for discounting are met could be a component of the liability that is reasonably estimable. Accordingly, it is possible for an entity to measure certain components of the liability on a discounted basis and measure other components of the liability on an undiscounted basis.

Because of the nature of environmental liabilities, as well as the long periods over which remediation costs are typically incurred, we generally would not expect the second criterion to be met. That is, it would generally be difficult for reporting entities to reliably determine the amount and timing of cash payments in future periods. Such an assessment should be based on objective and verifiable information.

With respect to the postremediation component of the environmental remediation liability, the costs incurred during this phase generally span a long period, which may or may not be specified by the EPA. Although the absence of a definitive required postremediation monitoring term makes it challenging to determine whether discounting is appropriate, we do not believe that such an absence would preclude discounting. Similarly, the need to estimate any inflation or productivity improvements does not, in itself, result in a conclusion that the cash flows are not reliably determinable. We believe that the AICPA Accounting Standards Executive Committee (the original developer of the guidance codified in ASC 410-30) contemplated situations in which discounting would be acceptable even though the amount or timing of cash payments is not known with certainty or precision. In that regard, on a continuum of probability, the "reliably determinable" standard is something less than "known with certainty or precision" but more than "reasonably estimable."

SEC Considerations

It is important to note that ASC 410-30 does not prescribe the particular discount rate to be used when a reporting entity determines that it is allowable and appropriate to discount an environmental remediation liability. However, ASC 410-30 refers to the SEC staff's interpretive guidance in SAB Topic 5.Y, Question 1 (codified in ASC 450-20-S99-1), on the discount rate to be used for measuring product or environmental remediation liabilities. That guidance states, in part:

> **Question 1:** Assuming that the registrant's estimate of an environmental remediation or product liability meets the conditions set forth in [ASC 410-30-35-12] for recognition on a discounted basis, what discount rate should be applied and what, if any, special disclosures are required in the notes to the financial statements?
>
> **Interpretive Response:** The rate used to discount the cash payments should be the rate that will produce an amount at which the environmental or product liability could be settled in an arm's-length transaction with a third party. Further, the discount rate used to discount the cash payments should not exceed the interest rate on monetary assets that are essentially risk free and have maturities comparable to that of the environmental or product liability. [Footnote omitted]

While the guidance above is applicable to SEC registrants, we believe that entities that are not SEC registrants should also consider this guidance.

3.4.4 Accounting for Potential Cost Recoveries

Under ASC 410-30-35-8, potential recoveries of environmental remediation costs may be claimed from various parties or sources, including insurers, other PRPs, and governmental or third-party entities. With respect to the impact of potential recoveries, ASC 410-30-35-8 states, in part:

> The amount of an environmental remediation liability should be determined independently from any potential claim for recovery, and an asset relating to the recovery shall be recognized only when realization of the claim for recovery is deemed probable. The term *probable* is used in [ASC 410-30] with the specific technical meaning in [ASC] 450-20-25-1.

The determination that a potential recovery is probable involves significant judgment and should be based on all relevant facts and circumstances. Paragraph C-28 of AICPA Statement of Position 96-1 (the guidance that was codified in ASC 410-30) states, in part:

> To evaluate whether the recovery of a potential claim is probable, correspondence or communication with others such as the insurer, PRPs other than participating PRPs, or legal counsel generally is necessary.

3.4.4.1 Potential Cost Recoveries From Insurance Carriers

With respect to potential cost recoveries from insurance carriers, management should consider both internal and external evidence regarding an insurance claim, including:

- Direct confirmation from the insurance carrier that it would agree with the claim.
- In the absence of direct evidence from the insurance carrier, an opinion from legal counsel that it is "probable," as that term is used in ASC 450, that:
  - The insurance policy is enforceable.
  - Any loss events are covered.
  - The insurance carrier will pay the claim.
- The insurance carrier's financial ability to pay the claim.

However, ASC 410-30-35-9 indicates that "[i]f the claim is the subject of litigation, a rebuttable presumption exists that realization of the claim is not probable."

 SEC Considerations

The guidance in ASC 410-30-35-9 is consistent with the SEC staff's interpretive guidance in Question 2 of SAB Topic 5.Y (codified in ASC 450-20-S99-1). Specifically, footnote 49 of that guidance, which addresses disclosures of uncertainties regarding the legal sufficiency of insurance claims or solvency of insurance carriers, states:

> The [SEC] staff believes there is a rebuttable presumption that no asset should be recognized for a claim for recovery from a party that is asserting that it is not liable to indemnify the registrant. Registrants that overcome that presumption should disclose the amount of recorded recoveries that are being contested and discuss the reasons for concluding that the amounts are probable of recovery.

3.4.4.2 *Potential Cost Recoveries From Other Entities*

Generally, claims made against entities other than insurance carriers for potential cost recoveries will be subject to litigation; therefore, there may be a presumption that recovery is not probable. Such a presumption may be difficult to overcome and would generally require, at a minimum, the opinion of competent legal counsel that recovery is probable.

If a reporting entity determines that a potential recovery is probable, it should record an asset for the expected recovery separately from the environmental remediation liability unless the criteria in ASC 210-20 for offsetting have been met. ASC 410-30-45-2 states that "[i]t would be rare, if ever, that the facts and circumstances surrounding environmental remediation liabilities and related receivables and potential recoveries would meet all of these conditions."

The recorded asset may be measured on a discounted or undiscounted basis depending on whether certain conditions are met, as illustrated in the flowchart below.

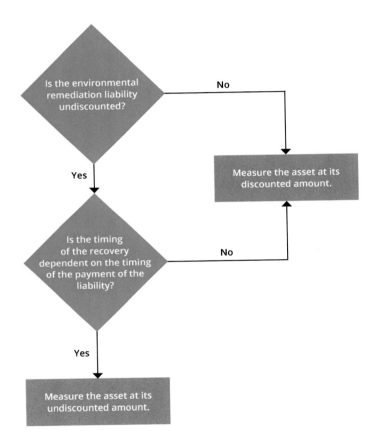

Regardless of whether the asset is measured at its discounted or undiscounted amount, it must be measured net of any transaction costs (e.g., legal fees) related to the receipt of the recovery.

3.5 Financial Statement Presentation

3.5.1 Balance Sheet Presentation

ASC 410-30

45-1 An entity's balance sheet may include several assets that relate to an environmental remediation obligation. Among them are the following:

a. Receivables from other potentially responsible parties that are not providing initial funding

b. Anticipated recoveries from insurers

c. Anticipated recoveries from prior owners as a result of indemnification agreements.

45-2 A debtor that has a right of setoff that meets all of the conditions in paragraph 210-20-45-1 may offset the related asset and liability and report the net amount. It would be rare, if ever, that the facts and circumstances surrounding environmental remediation liabilities and related receivables and potential recoveries would meet all of these conditions.

With respect to the balance sheet, a reporting entity should present a liability for its allocable share of the environmental remediation costs (see Sections 3.3 through 3.3.2.3 for a discussion of how those costs should be measured and allocated). If the reporting entity prepares a classified balance sheet, the environmental remediation liability should be bifurcated into current and noncurrent portions on the basis of the expected timing of settlement.

In addition, as discussed in the guidance above, several assets related to an environmental remediation obligation may be presented in a reporting entity's balance sheet. These assets should be presented separately from the liability (i.e., they should not be netted against the liability) unless the criteria in ASC 210-20-45-1 (reproduced below) are met.

ASC 210-20

45-1 A right of setoff exists when all of the following conditions are met:

a. Each of two parties owes the other determinable amounts.

b. The reporting party has the right to set off the amount owed with the amount owed by the other party.

c. The reporting party intends to set off.

d. The right of setoff is enforceable at law.

We believe that with respect to environmental obligations, it would be rare for a reporting entity to conclude that all of the above conditions are met. Specifically, the first criterion contemplates that the asset and liability are with the same counterparty. In the context of environmental obligations, the reporting entity's liability is typically to the EPA or another state or federal governmental agency, while its assets are recoverable from another entity, such as another PRP or an insurance company. Therefore, it would generally not be appropriate for an entity to offset assets and liabilities related to an environmental remediation obligation in the balance sheet.

3.5.2 Income Statement Presentation

With respect to income statement presentation, ASC 410-30-45-4 states that environmental costs should be presented as operating expenses because "the events underlying the incurrence of the obligation relate to an entity's operations." In addition, ASC 410-30-45-4 indicates that any credits recorded as a result of probable recoveries should be presented in the same line item as the environmental costs. We believe that when a reporting entity discounts its environmental remediation liability, the expense resulting from accretion of the liability to its undiscounted value should be classified as an additional operating cost of the remediation effort rather than as interest expense. Similarly, we believe that when a reporting entity discounts an asset for probable recoveries, the income resulting from accretion of the asset to its undiscounted value should be classified as operating income rather than interest income.

3.6 Disclosure Considerations

3.6.1 Interaction of ASC 410-30 With ASC 450-20 and ASC 275

ASC 410-30-50-5 states that ASC 450-20 provides the primary disclosure requirements for environmental remediation loss contingencies. In addition, ASC 410-30-50-6 states that the incremental disclosure requirements of ASC 275 also apply to environmental remediation liabilities. The table below summarizes the application of the disclosure requirements of ASC 450-20 and ASC 275 to environmental liabilities.

Disclosures Related to Loss Contingencies		
Possibility That a Loss Has Been Incurred	Ability to Estimate a Loss	Disclosure Requirements of ASC 450-20 and ASC 275
Reasonably possible	May or may not be reasonably estimable	Disclose all of the following: • "The nature of the contingency" (i.e., a description of the environmental remediation obligation). See ASC 450-20-50-4(a). • "An estimate of the possible loss or range of loss or a statement that such an estimate cannot be made." See ASC 450-20-50-4(b). • A statement indicating that it is at least reasonably possible that the estimated amount of the loss will change in the near term if (1) it is at least reasonably possible that the estimate will change in the near term and (2) the effect of the change would be material. See ASC 275-10-50-8.
Probable	Not reasonably estimable	Disclose both of the following: • "The nature of the contingency" (i.e., a description of the environmental remediation obligation). See ASC 450-20-50-4(a). • A statement that the amount of the loss cannot be reasonably estimated. See ASC 450-20-50-4(b).

Probable	Reasonably estimable	Disclose all of the following:
		
		• "The nature of the contingency" (i.e., a description of the environmental remediation obligation). "The term *reserve* shall not be used for an accrual made pursuant to [ASC] 450-20-25-2; that term is limited to an amount of unidentified or unsegregated assets held or retained for a specific purpose." See ASC 450-20-50-1 and ASC 450-20-50-4(a).
		• The total amount of the loss that has been recognized (if such disclosure is required to ensure that the financial statements are not misleading). See ASC 450-20-50-1.
		• A statement indicating that it is at least reasonably possible that the estimated amount of the loss will change in the near term if (1) it is at least reasonably possible that the estimate will change in the near term and (2) the effect of the change would be material. See ASC 275-10-50-8.
		• The exposure to loss in excess of the amount accrued under ASC 410-30 if there is at least a reasonable possibility that such excess loss may have been incurred. The disclosure should include both of the following:
		   ◦ The nature of the contingency.
		   ◦ An estimate of the possible loss or range of loss or a statement that such an estimate cannot be made. See ASC 450-20-50-3 and 50-4.

3.6.2 Other Required Disclosures Under ASC 410-30

ASC 410-30 requires certain disclosures in addition to the applicable disclosures prescribed by ASC 450-20 and ASC 275. Those additional required disclosures are summarized in the table below.

Topic	Other Required Disclosures Under ASC 410-30
Unasserted claims	"Whether notification by regulatory authorities . . . constitutes the assertion of a claim is a matter of legal determination. If an entity concludes that it has no current legal obligation to remediate a situation of probable or possible environmental impact, then . . . no disclosure is required. However, if an entity is required by existing laws and regulations to report the release of hazardous substances and to begin a remediation study or if assertion of a claim is deemed probable, the matter would represent a loss contingency subject to the disclosure provisions of [ASC 450-20-50-3 and 50-4], regardless of a lack of involvement by a regulatory agency." See ASC 410-30-50-13.

Discounted or undiscounted liabilities	Disclose all of the following:
	• Whether environmental liabilities are measured on a discounted basis. See ASC 410-30-50-4 and ASC 410-30-50-7.
	• If any portion of a recognized environmental remediation liability is discounted:
	  ○ The "undiscounted amount of the obligation."
	  ○ The "discount rate used in the present-value determinations." See ASC 410-30-50-7.

Losses arising after the date of the financial statements	If the accrual of such losses is not required, disclosure may be necessary to ensure that the financial statements are not misleading. If such disclosure is necessary, it should include both of the following: • The nature of the contingency (i.e., a description of the environmental remediation obligation). See ASC 450-20-50-9. • An estimate of the possible loss exposure or a statement that such an estimate cannot be made. See ASC 450-20-50-9.

SEC Considerations

The requirements of ASC 410-30-50-7 to disclose the undiscounted amount of an environmental remediation liability and the discount rate used are consistent with the SEC staff's interpretive response to Question 1 of SAB Topic 5.Y. However, that interpretive response also requires disclosure of both of the following:

- "[E]xpected payments for each of the five succeeding years and the aggregate amount thereafter."
- A "reconciliation of the expected aggregate undiscounted amount to amounts recognized in the statements of financial position."

In addition, the interpretive response to Question 1 of SAB Topic 5.Y states that "[m]aterial changes in the expected aggregate amount since the prior balance sheet date, other than those resulting from pay-down of the obligation, should be explained."

See Section 3.6.4 for a discussion of additional SEC disclosure requirements related to environmental obligations.

Connecting the Dots

ASC 410-30-50-14 acknowledges that in certain situations, the estimated total unrecognized exposure to environmental remediation loss contingencies may not have a material adverse effect on the consolidated financial statements. In such situations, it may be appropriate for a reporting entity to provide a disclosure that addresses this exposure in total. ASC 410-30-50-14 provides the following example of such a disclosure:

> [M]anagement believes that the outcome of these uncertainties should not have [or "may have"] a material adverse effect on the financial condition, cash flows, or operating results of the entity.

However, as noted in ASC 410-30-50-15, this type of disclosure should not be considered a substitute for any of the required disclosures discussed above.

3.6.3 Disclosures That Are Encouraged but Not Required

Because of the pervasive uncertainty associated with many environmental remediation obligations and the significant judgment required in accounting for such obligations, certain additional disclosures are encouraged, but not required, under ASC 410-30-50. Those encouraged disclosures are summarized in the table below.

Topic	Disclosures Encouraged, but Not Required, Under ASC 410-30-50
Environmental liabilities — general	• The "event, situation, or set of circumstances that generally triggers recognition of loss contingencies that arise out of the entity's environmental remediation-related obligations (for example, during or upon completion of the [FS])." See ASC 410-30-50-8. • "The estimated time frame of disbursements for recorded amounts if expenditures are expected to continue over the long term." See ASC 410-30-50-10(a). • "If an estimate of the probable or reasonably possible loss or range of loss cannot be made, the reasons why it cannot be made." See ASC 410-30-50-10(c). • The "estimated time frame for resolution of the uncertainty as to the amount of the loss." See ASC 410-30-50-11. • "The amount recognized [in the income statement] for environmental remediation loss contingencies in each period." See ASC 410-30-50-12(a). • "The income statement caption in which environmental remediation costs . . . are included." See ASC 410-30-50-12(c).
Environmental liabilities — site-specific	If information related to an individual site is relevant to the assessment of the reporting entity's statement of financial position, the following disclosures under ASC 410-30-50-10(d) are encouraged with respect to the site: • "The total amount accrued for the site." • "The nature of any reasonably possible loss contingency or additional loss, and an estimate of the possible loss or the fact that an estimate cannot be made and the reasons why it cannot be made." • "Whether other [PRPs] are involved and the entity's estimated share of the obligation." • "The status of regulatory proceedings." • "The estimated time frame for resolution of the contingency."

(Table continued)

Topic	Disclosures Encouraged, but Not Required, Under ASC 410-30-50
Cost recoveries	<ul><li>The reporting entity's "policy concerning the timing of recognition of recoveries." See ASC 410-30-50-8.</li><li>"The estimated time frame for realization of recognized probable recoveries, if realization is not expected in the near term." See ASC 410-30-50-10(b).</li><li>"The amount of any recovery from third parties that is credited to environmental remediation costs in each period." See ASC 410-30-50-12(b).</li><li>The income statement caption in which credits related to third-party recoveries are included. See ASC 410-30-50-12(c).</li></ul>

3.6.4 SEC Disclosure Requirements

While the guidance in ASC 410-30-50 only *encourages* disclosure of the items described in Section 3.6.3 above, the interpretive response to Question 2 of SAB Topic 5.Y indicates that the SEC staff typically *requires* disclosure of these items to "prevent the financial statements from being misleading and to inform readers fully regarding the range of reasonably possible outcomes that could have a material effect on the registrant's financial condition, results of operations, or liquidity."

That interpretive response also states that in addition to the disclosures required under ASC 410-30 and ASC 450-20, other disclosures may be necessary, including the following:

- "Circumstances affecting the reliability and precision of loss estimates."

- "The extent to which unasserted claims are reflected in any accrual or may affect the magnitude of the contingency."

- "Uncertainties with respect to joint and several liability that may affect the magnitude of the contingency, including disclosure of the aggregate expected cost to remediate particular sites that are individually material if the likelihood of contribution by the other significant parties has not been established."

- "Disclosure of the nature and terms of cost-sharing arrangements with other [PRPs]."

- "The extent to which disclosed but unrecognized contingent losses are expected to be recoverable through insurance, indemnification arrangements, or other sources, with disclosure of any material limitations of that recovery."

- "Uncertainties regarding the legal sufficiency of insurance claims or solvency of insurance carriers."

- "The time frame over which the accrued or presently unrecognized amounts may be paid out."

- "Material components of the accruals and significant assumptions underlying estimates."

Further, the interpretive response to Question 2 of SAB Topic 5.Y cautions registrants that a disclosure that "the contingency is not expected to be material does not satisfy the requirements of [ASC 450] if there is at least a reasonable possibility that a loss exceeding amounts already recognized may have been incurred and the amount of that additional loss would be material to a decision to buy or sell the registrant's securities. In that case, the registrant must either (a) disclose the estimated additional loss, or range of loss, that is reasonably possible, or (b) state that such an estimate cannot be made."

In its interpretive response to Question 3 of SAB Topic 5.Y, the SEC staff addresses disclosures that may be required outside the financial statements and states, in part:

> Registrants should consider the requirements of Items 101 (Description of Business), 103 (Legal Proceedings), and 303 (MD&A) of Regulation S-K. The Commission has issued interpretive releases that provide additional guidance with respect to these items. In a 1989 interpretive release, the Commission noted that the availability of insurance, indemnification, or contribution may be relevant in determining whether the criteria for disclosure have been met with respect to a contingency. The registrant's assessment in this regard should include consideration of facts such as the periods in which claims for recovery may be realized, the likelihood that the claims may be contested, and the financial condition of third parties from which recovery is expected.

> Disclosures made pursuant to the guidance identified in the preceding paragraph should be sufficiently specific to enable a reader to understand the scope of the contingencies affecting the registrant. For example, a registrant's discussion of historical and anticipated environmental expenditures should, to the extent material, describe separately (a) recurring costs associated with managing hazardous substances and pollution in on-going operations, (b) capital expenditures to limit or monitor hazardous substances or pollutants, (c) mandated expenditures to remediate previously contaminated sites, and (d) other infrequent or non-recurring clean-up expenditures that can be anticipated but which are not required in the present circumstances. Disaggregated disclosure that describes accrued and reasonably likely losses with respect to particular environmental sites that are individually material may be necessary for a full understanding of these contingencies. Also, if management's investigation of potential liability and remediation cost is at different stages with respect to individual sites, the consequences of this with respect to amounts accrued and disclosed should be discussed. [Footnotes omitted]

Chapter 4 — Accounting for Asset Retirement Obligations

This chapter provides an overview of the accounting and disclosure requirements for AROs in ASC 410-20, along with certain interpretive guidance on applying the scope, initial recognition, initial measurement, and subsequent measurement provisions of this accounting guidance. Chapter 5 then provides examples of AROs commonly encountered in certain industries, along with a discussion of accounting and financial reporting issues that companies in those industries commonly encounter when accounting for such AROs.

4.1 Overview of ASC 410-20

ASC 410-20 provides the relevant guidance on accounting for AROs and generally applies to "[l]egal obligations associated with the retirement of a tangible long-lived asset that result from the acquisition, construction, or development and (or) the normal operation of a long-lived asset" (ASC 410-20-15-2). An ARO is recognized when incurred if a reasonable estimate of fair value can be made, and it should be initially measured at fair value. If its fair value cannot be reasonably estimated, the ARO should be recognized when a reasonable estimate of fair value can be made.

When initially recognizing an ARO, an entity should capitalize the asset retirement cost by increasing the long-lived asset's carrying value by the same amount as the ARO. Subsequently, changes to the ARO should be recognized for changes due to the passage of time (accretion of the ARO) and revisions to either the timing or the amount of the original estimate of cash flows used for measuring the fair value of the liability. The entity should recognize changes due to the passage of time as an operating expense and an increase to the ARO by applying an interest method allocation to the ARO at the beginning of the period, using the credit-adjusted risk-free rate at the time the initial ARO was recognized and measured. Changes in subsequent measurement of the ARO resulting from revisions to the estimated timing or amount of cash flows should be recognized as an increase or decrease in the carrying amount of the ARO and the related long-lived asset. The entity should measure increases in estimated cash flows by using the current credit-adjusted risk-free rate (creating an additional "layer" of the ARO), and it should measure decreases in estimated cash flows by using the credit-adjusted risk-free rate that existed when the ARO was initially recognized. In addition, the entity should subsequently recognize as expense (depreciate) the amount capitalized as part of the cost of the related long-lived asset by using a systematic and rational method over the long-lived asset's economic useful life.

Application of the guidance in ASC 410-20 can be complex and requires significant management estimates and judgment. The sections below further discuss the scope of ASC 410-20 as well as the initial and subsequent recognition and measurement provisions of this guidance, including some of the practical challenges that entities may encounter in applying those provisions.

4.2 Scope of ASC 410-20

ASC 410-20

15-2 The guidance in this Subtopic applies to the following transactions and activities:

a. Legal obligations associated with the retirement of a tangible long-lived asset that result from the acquisition, construction, or development and (or) the normal operation of a long-lived asset, including any legal obligations that require disposal of a replaced part that is a component of a tangible long-lived asset.

b. An environmental remediation liability that results from the normal operation of a long-lived asset and that is associated with the retirement of that asset. The fact that partial settlement of an obligation is required or performed before full retirement of an asset does not remove that obligation from the scope of this Subtopic. If environmental contamination is incurred in the normal operation of a long-lived asset and is associated with the retirement of that asset, then this Subtopic will apply (and Subtopic 410-30 will not apply) if the entity is legally obligated to treat the contamination.

c. A conditional obligation to perform a retirement activity. Uncertainty about the timing of settlement of the asset retirement obligation does not remove that obligation from the scope of this Subtopic but will affect the measurement of a liability for that obligation (see paragraph 410-20-25-10).

d. Obligations of a lessor in connection with leased property that meet the provisions in (a). Paragraph 840-10-25-16 requires that lease classification tests performed in accordance with the requirements of Subtopic 840-10 incorporate the requirements of this Subtopic to the extent applicable.

e. The costs associated with the retirement of a specified asset that qualifies as historical waste equipment as defined by EU Directive 2002/96/EC. (See paragraphs 410-20-55-23 through 55-30 and Example 4 [paragraph 410-20-55-63] for illustration of this guidance.) Paragraph 410-20-55-24 explains how the Directive distinguishes between new and historical waste and provides related implementation guidance.

Pending Content (ASC 410-20) Transition Guidance: 842-10-65-1

15-2 The guidance in this Subtopic applies to the following transactions and activities:

a. Legal obligations associated with the retirement of a tangible long-lived asset that result from the acquisition, construction, or development and (or) the normal operation of a long-lived asset, including any legal obligations that require disposal of a replaced part that is a component of a tangible long-lived asset.

b. An environmental remediation liability that results from the normal operation of a long-lived asset and that is associated with the retirement of that asset. The fact that partial settlement of an obligation is required or performed before full retirement of an asset does not remove that obligation from the scope of this Subtopic. If environmental contamination is incurred in the normal operation of a long-lived asset and is associated with the retirement of that asset, then this Subtopic will apply (and Subtopic 410-30 will not apply) if the entity is legally obligated to treat the contamination.

c. A conditional obligation to perform a retirement activity. Uncertainty about the timing of settlement of the asset retirement obligation does not remove that obligation from the scope of this Subtopic but will affect the measurement of a liability for that obligation (see paragraph 410-20-25-10).

d. Obligations of a lessor in connection with an underlying asset that meet the provisions in (a).

e. The costs associated with the retirement of a specified asset that qualifies as historical waste equipment as defined by EU Directive 2002/96/EC. (See paragraphs 410-20-55-23 through 55-30 and Example 4 [paragraph 410-20-55-63] for illustration of this guidance.) Paragraph 410-20-55-24 explains how the Directive distinguishes between new and historical waste and provides related implementation guidance.

ASC 410-20 applies to legal obligations associated with the retirement of a tangible long-lived asset. The determination of whether a legal obligation exists should generally be clear and unambiguous. However, ASC 410-20 acknowledges in defining the term "legal obligation" that such an obligation can be established by an existing or enacted law, statute, ordinance, or written or oral contract, or pursuant to the doctrine of promissory estoppel. If an entity makes a promise to a third party, including the public at large, about its intentions to undertake asset retirement activities, significant judgment may be required in the determination of whether the entity has created a legal obligation under the legal doctrine of promissory estoppel, which is defined as the "principle that a promise made without consideration may nonetheless be enforced to prevent injustice if the promisor should have reasonably expected the promisee to rely on the promise and if the promisee did actually rely on the promise to his or her detriment."[1]

The implementation guidance in ASC 410-20-55-2 provides the following example of a legal obligation that may be established under the doctrine of promissory estoppel:

> ### ASC 410-20
>
> **55-2** [A]ssume an entity operates a manufacturing facility and has plans to retire it within five years. Members of the local press have begun to publicize the fact that when the entity ceases operations at the plant, it plans to abandon the site without demolishing the building and restoring the underlying land. Due to the significant negative publicity and demands by the public that the entity commit to dismantling the plant upon retirement, the entity's chief executive officer holds a press conference at city hall to announce that the entity will demolish the building and restore the underlying land when the entity ceases operations at the plant. Although no law, statute, ordinance, or written contract exists requiring the entity to perform any demolition or restoration activities, the promise made by the entity's chief executive officer may have created a legal obligation under the doctrine of promissory estoppel. In that circumstance, the entity's management (and legal counsel, if necessary) would have to evaluate the particular facts and circumstances to determine whether a legal obligation exists.

A company's past practice also may, but does not necessarily, create a legal obligation. For example, a utility company may regularly remove and replace utility poles as part of its normal operations, thereby potentially creating an expectation that it will continue to do so. This expectation may create a legal obligation based on the principle of promissory estoppel.[2] For rate-regulated entities (such as public utilities), recovery through rates of future removal costs alone does not create an ARO. However, rate-regulated entities should review the applicable regulatory proceedings to determine whether a promise to remove an asset was made for the regulator to approve the recovery of costs in rates. If such an agreement was made and if the promisee relied on it to his or her detriment, this may create an ARO through promissory estoppel.

Connecting the Dots

In determining whether an entity has a legal obligation under the notion of promissory estoppel, entities must work closely with legal counsel to evaluate their own specific facts and circumstances. When this determination is unclear, entities may wish to obtain a legal opinion to support their conclusions.

Entities should evaluate the existence of legal obligations on the basis of current laws, regulations, contractual obligations, and related interpretations and facts and circumstances and should not forecast changes in laws or interpretations of such laws and regulations. The impacts of changes in laws or regulations should be considered in the period in which such laws or regulations are enacted.

---

[1] See ASC 410-20-20, which cites the definition used in *Black's Law Dictionary*, seventh edition.
[2] Wood utility poles used in certain industries are typically treated with certain chemicals and, once removed, are subject to special disposal requirements under existing legislation. In these circumstances, the special disposal procedures under existing legislation create an ARO for the disposal of the utility poles once removed, which should be accounted for under the guidance in ASC 410-20 regardless of whether the removal or replacement of the utility poles is considered an ARO under the doctrine of promissory estoppel. See ASC 410-20-55-49 through 55-52.

Connecting the Dots

The enactment date is the date on which all steps in the process for legislation to become law have been completed (e.g., in the United States, the date the president signs the legislation and it becomes law). For rules and regulations issued by federal regulatory agencies to implement enacted U.S. laws, the enactment date is generally the date on which final rules or regulations promulgated by the federal regulatory agency are published in the *Federal Register*, which may differ from the effective date of such rules or regulations. Entities may need to exercise considerable judgment and obtain the assistance of legal counsel in determining (1) the enactment date of laws and regulations implemented in jurisdictions outside the United States or (2) when regulations issued by governmental agencies to implement and interpret these laws are enacted.

The determination that a legal obligation exists is not affected by expectations of nonenforcement, or uncertainty about enforcement, of existing laws, regulations, or contractual provisions by governmental agencies or other third parties. However, an entity would consider such expectations or uncertainty when measuring an ARO by using an expected present value technique (see guidance on initial and subsequent measurement of ARO liabilities in Sections 4.4 and 4.5). An entity may need to use significant judgment when determining whether it has a legal obligation within the scope of ASC 410-20, and it may be required to seek input from legal and other professional advisers in making this determination.

Many component parts of larger systems have special disposal requirements, but there may not be a legal requirement to retire or remove the larger system to which the component parts belong. The costs associated with the legal obligation for disposal of a component part are within the scope of ASC 410-20 even though there is no legal obligation to remove the larger system. However, the cost of the replacement parts and their installation is not included in the measurement and recognition of the ARO. Further, if there is no legal obligation to remove the component part, removal costs would not be within the scope of ASC 410-20; only the disposal costs associated with the obligation to dispose of the contaminated component part, once retired and removed, are within the scope of ASC 410-20. ASC 410-20-55-10 includes the following example of component parts that wear out after a period and are subject to a special (legal) disposal requirement when removed:

ASC 410-20

55-10 [C]onsider an aluminum smelter that owns and operates several kilns lined with a special type of brick. The kilns have a long useful life, but the bricks wear out after approximately five years of use and are replaced on a periodic basis to maintain optimal efficiency of the kilns. Because the bricks become contaminated with hazardous chemicals while in the kiln, a state law requires that when the bricks are removed, they must be disposed of at a special hazardous waste site. The obligation to dispose of those bricks is within the scope of this Subtopic. The cost of the replacement bricks and their installation are not part of that obligation. . . .

4.2.1 Application of ASC 410-20 to Environmental Remediation Liabilities

The scope of ASC 410-20 is limited to those obligations that cannot be realistically avoided, assuming that the asset is operated in accordance with its intended use (i.e., resulting from the normal operation of a long-lived asset). Contamination arising out of "normal" operations generally is expected or predictable, gradual (or occurring over time), integral to operations, or unavoidable and does not require an immediate response. Contamination arising out of improper use of an asset or a catastrophic event is generally unexpected, requires immediate response or reporting, generally could have been controlled or mitigated, and is the result of a failure in equipment or noncompliance with company procedures. If an environmental remediation obligation is the result of the improper operation of an asset or the result of a catastrophic event, it would be subject to the provisions of ASC 410-30 or ASC 450, which address the accounting for environmental obligations and contingencies, respectively.

See Chapter 1 for further discussion about the determination of whether an environmental remediation liability is within the scope of ASC 410-20 or ASC 410-30.

4.2.2 Application of ASC 410-20 to Leases

ASC 410-20 applies to AROs of a lessor in connection with a leased property. ASC 410-20 also applies to obligations of a lessee in connection with leased property, regardless of whether imposed by the lease agreement or by a party other than the lessor, if those obligations do not meet the definition of either minimum lease payments or contingent rentals under the guidance in ASC 840-10. If the lessee obligations represent minimum or contingent rentals, they should be accounted for by the lessee in accordance with ASC 840. As discussed in greater detail below, lessee obligations accounted for under ASC 410-20 are initially measured at fair value, and uncertainties associated with the likelihood that the lessor will enforce a lease provision are incorporated into the fair value measurement of the obligation. Under ASC 840, minimum lease payments affect initial lease classification (operating vs. capital) and subsequent accounting for leases by the lessee (the measurement of obligations under leases in accordance with the guidance in ASC 840 is not based on fair value; therefore, any uncertainties associated with the likelihood that the lessor will enforce a lease provision or require the payments are not considered in the measurement of the lessee's obligations under ASC 840).

At times, it may be challenging to distinguish between lessee obligations that meet the definition of minimum lease payments or contingent rentals and those that do not. In a speech at the 2003 AICPA National Conference on Current SEC Developments, the SEC staff acknowledged that diversity in practice exists in accounting for obligations to retire a leased asset. The staff stated in the speech that it generally has not objected to accounting for such obligations under either ASC 840 or ASC 410-20 as long as the accounting policy is applied consistently. In addition, the staff indicated in the speech that it believes that retirement obligations accounted for under ASC 840 should not be treated as contingent rentals since the staff does not believe that such obligations meet the definition of contingent rentals.

Notwithstanding the views expressed in the SEC staff's speech, and in the absence of an entity's consistently applied accounting policy election, we generally believe that the determination of whether an obligation to retire (or bear the cost of retiring) a leased asset should be accounted for as a minimum lease payment or as an ARO is a matter of judgment based on analysis of the relevant facts and circumstances. ASC 840-10-25-5 defines minimum lease payments from the standpoint of the lessee as "the payments that the lessee is obligated to make or can be required to make in connection with the leased property." Therefore, as a general rule, if the obligation is directly related to the leased asset or to a component of the leased asset, the lessee should account for the obligation in accordance with ASC 840. If the obligation either is related to assets (e.g., office equipment, machinery) placed in service by the lessee at the leased premises or constitutes improvements made to the leased property by the lessee during the lease term (i.e., leasehold improvements that are owned by the lessee), the lessee should generally account for the obligation as an ARO in accordance with ASC 410-20.

Changing Lanes

In February 2016, the FASB issued ASU 2016-02, its new standard on accounting for leases. When the guidance in the ASU becomes effective, it will replace existing lease accounting guidance in ASC 840 with ASC 842. ASC 842 will be effective for public entities for fiscal years beginning after December 15, 2018, and for nonpublic entities for periods beginning after December 15, 2019. ASC 842 does not significantly amend the scope of ASC 410-20 with respect to lessor and lessee AROs. However, the following content (codified in ASC 842-10-55-37) will be added upon the adoption of ASU 2016-02:

> Obligations imposed by a lease agreement to return an underlying asset to its original condition if it has been modified by the lessee (for example, a requirement to remove a lessee-installed leasehold improvement) generally would not meet the definition of lease payments or variable lease payments and would be accounted for in accordance with Subtopic 410-20 on asset retirement and environmental obligations. In contrast, costs to dismantle and remove an underlying asset at the end of the lease term that are imposed by the lease agreement generally would be considered lease payments or variable lease payments.

Accordingly, after the adoption of ASC 842, entities should apply this guidance when evaluating whether obligations imposed by a lease agreement should be accounted for under ASC 410-20 or ASC 842. For additional guidance, see Deloitte's *A Roadmap to Applying the New Leasing Standard*.

4.3 Initial Recognition of AROs and Asset Retirement Costs

ASC 410-20

25-4 An entity shall recognize the fair value of a liability for an asset retirement obligation in the period in which it is incurred if a reasonable estimate of fair value can be made. If a reasonable estimate of fair value cannot be made in the period the asset retirement obligation is incurred, the liability shall be recognized when a reasonable estimate of fair value can be made. If a tangible long-lived asset with an existing asset retirement obligation is acquired, a liability for that obligation shall be recognized at the asset's acquisition date as if that obligation were incurred on that date.

25-5 Upon initial recognition of a liability for an asset retirement obligation, an entity shall capitalize an asset retirement cost by increasing the carrying amount of the related long-lived asset by the same amount as the liability. Paragraph 835-20-30-5 explains that capitalized asset retirement costs do not qualify as expenditures for purposes of applying Subtopic 835-20.

Entities are required to recognize the fair value of a liability for an ARO in the period in which it is incurred if a reasonable estimate of fair value can be made. If such a reasonable estimate cannot be made, recognition should occur when a reasonable estimate of fair value can be made. An obligation to perform asset retirement activities is unconditional, and an ARO should be measured and recognized regardless of whether (1) there is uncertainty about the timing or method of settlement or (2) such timing and method of settlement are conditional on a future event. Entities would factor this uncertainty into the measurement of the fair value of the ARO by using an expected present value technique. Significant judgment will often be required in the determination of whether sufficient information is available to measure the fair value of an ARO.

ASC 410-20-25-6 states that sufficient information exists to reasonably estimate the fair value of an ARO in the following situations:

- When it is evident that the fair value of the ARO has been included in the purchase price of the asset.

- When an active market exists for the transfer of the ARO to a third party.
- When there is sufficient information to apply an expected present value technique discussed in ASC 820-10-55-4 through 55-20.

ASC 410-20-25-8 expands on the last situation above by discussing the circumstances in which an entity would have sufficient information to apply an expected present value technique. Those circumstances include either of the following:

- When the settlement date and method of settlement for the obligation have been specified in the law, regulation, or contract that gives rise to the ARO.
- When information is available to reasonably estimate (1) the "settlement date or the range of potential settlement dates," (2) the "method of settlement or potential methods of settlement," and (3) the "probabilities associated with the potential settlement dates and potential methods of settlement."

With respect to the second circumstance above, ASC 410-20-25-11 indicates that to estimate potential settlement dates, potential methods of settlement, and the related probabilities, an entity should consider the following:

- *Entity's past practice* — At what point and how often have similar assets been retired in the past? What method was used to retire them?
- *Industry practice* — At what point and how often have the entity's competitors retired similar assets? What methods did the entity's competitors use to retire them?
- *Management's intent* — Is there a plan to retire or dispose of the asset?
- *Estimated economic life* — What is the asset's estimated economic life? Does management plan on maintaining the asset to extend its estimated economic life? Will technological advances render the asset obsolete before the end of its economic life?

Connecting the Dots

We believe that entities would typically have sufficient information to estimate a range of potential settlement dates, the potential methods of settlement, and the related probabilities on the basis of an analysis of the factors listed above. It would not be appropriate for an entity to delay recognition of the liability merely on the basis that management does not intend to perform the asset retirement activities in the foreseeable future. ASC 410-20-25-8 clarifies that the timing of liability recognition under ASC 410-20 should not be based on when the retirement activities are probable of being performed (an ASC 450 approach); rather, any uncertainty with respect to timing of settlement should be incorporated into the measurement of the obligation.

An entity that believes that it lacks sufficient information to reasonably estimate the fair value of an ARO liability must have evidence to support that assertion. For example, evidence may include a history of indefinitely extending the economic lives of other long-lived assets that are the same as or similar to the assets under the related ARO by regularly repairing and maintaining the assets. In the rare circumstances in which sufficient information does not exist, an entity must disclose that fact and the reasons why an estimate could not be made, in accordance with ASC 410-20-50-2.

Under ASC 410-20-25-6, an entity is also required to identify all AROs. Therefore, it would be inappropriate for an entity to assert that the information to reasonably estimate fair value is insufficient simply because a thorough inventory of existing AROs has not been compiled.

ASC 410-20-25-8 also addresses uncertainty with regard to estimating a range of potential cash flows associated with the AROs identified by an entity. Generally, it would be inappropriate for an entity to assert that the information to reasonably estimate fair value is insufficient because of uncertainty about the costs of performing the asset retirement activities. This is supported by paragraph B23 of the Background Information and Basis for Conclusions of FASB Interpretation 47 (an interpretation of FASB Statement 143, which is the primary guidance codified in ASC 410-20), which states, in part:

> The Board concluded that an entity would generally have the ability to estimate a range of potential cash flows based on the current costs to perform the asset retirement activities under different methods of settlement that are currently available to the entity.

If an entity believes that sufficient information does not exist to reasonably estimate the fair value of an ARO, it should consider consulting with its independent auditors to ensure the appropriateness of that conclusion.

As required by ASC 410-20-25-5, upon initial recognition of an ARO, entities should capitalize an asset retirement cost by increasing the carrying value of the related tangible long-lived asset by the same amount as the liability. The example below illustrates the accounting entry to record upon initial recognition of an ARO.

Example 4-1

Company ABC has a new long-lived asset with an estimated useful life of 15 years. The ARO is calculated at acquisition, and the undiscounted cash flows in year 15 are determined to be $75,000. The present value of the ARO at acquisition is $22,060, which is based on a discount rate of 8.5 percent, the risk-free rate as adjusted for ABC's credit standing. Company ABC would initially record the following journal entry to reflect this ARO:

Long-lived asset (asset retirement cost)	22,060	
ARO		22,060

Over the 15-year useful life, ABC will accrete the liability each year by using the rate of 8.5 percent determined at acquisition. The accretion will result in a debit to operating expense (i.e., accretion expense) and a credit to the ARO liability. After 15 years, provided that there are no changes to ABC's initial assumptions, the total liability should be reflected at $75,000.

4.4 Initial Measurement of AROs and Asset Retirement Costs

ASC 410-20

30-1 An expected present value technique will usually be the only appropriate technique with which to estimate the fair value of a liability for an asset retirement obligation. An entity, when using that technique, shall discount the expected cash flows using a credit-adjusted risk-free rate. Thus, the effect of an entity's credit standing is reflected in the discount rate rather than in the expected cash flows. Proper application of a discount rate adjustment technique entails analysis of at least two liabilities — the liability that exists in the marketplace and has an observable interest rate and the liability being measured. The appropriate rate of interest for the cash flows being measured shall be inferred from the observable rate of interest of some other liability, and to draw that inference the characteristics of the cash flows shall be similar to those of the liability being measured. Rarely, if ever, would there be an observable rate of interest for a liability that has cash flows similar to an asset retirement obligation being measured. In addition, an asset retirement obligation usually will have uncertainties in both timing and amount. In that circumstance, employing a discount rate adjustment technique, where uncertainty is incorporated into the rate, will be difficult, if not impossible. See paragraphs 410-20-55-13 through 55-17 and Example 2 (paragraph 410-20-55-35). For further information on present value techniques, see the guidance beginning in paragraph 820-10-55-4.

AROs are initially measured at fair value. Given the lack of active markets for the transfer of such obligations, an expected present value technique will usually be the only appropriate technique with which to estimate the fair value of an ARO, which entails first estimating probability-weighted expected cash flows and then discounting such expected cash flows by using a credit-adjusted risk-free interest rate. ASC 410-20-55-13 provides the following implementation guidance related to the use of an expected present value technique:

ASC 410-20

55-13 This implementation guidance illustrates paragraph 410-20-30-1. In estimating the fair value of a liability for an asset retirement obligation using an expected present value technique, an entity shall begin by estimating the expected cash flows that reflect, to the extent possible, a marketplace assessment of the cost and timing of performing the required retirement activities. Considerations in estimating those expected cash flows include developing and incorporating explicit assumptions, to the extent possible, about all of the following:

a. The costs that a third party would incur in performing the tasks necessary to retire the asset

b. Other amounts that a third party would include in determining the price of the transfer, including, for example, inflation, overhead, equipment charges, profit margin, and advances in technology

c. The extent to which the amount of a third party's costs or the timing of its costs would vary under different future scenarios and the relative probabilities of those scenarios

d. The price that a third party would demand and could expect to receive for bearing the uncertainties and unforeseeable circumstances inherent in the obligation, sometimes referred to as a market-risk premium.

Measuring the fair value of an ARO requires many significant management estimates and judgments and poses several practical challenges for preparers of financial statements. Sections 4.4.1 and 4.4.2 below highlight a few of these challenges and provide guidance to help preparers address these challenges.

4.4.1 Determining an Appropriate Discount Rate

The credit-adjusted risk-free rate referred to in ASC 410-20-30-1 (reproduced above) represents a risk-free interest rate adjusted for the effect of an entity's credit standing, taking into consideration the effects of all terms, collateral, and existing guarantees on the fair value of the liability. Generally, the yield curve for U.S. Treasury securities, with a maturity matched to the expected timing of settlement of the ARO, is used to establish the appropriate risk-free rate for determining the credit-adjusted risk-free rate, even in periods when yields on U.S. Treasury notes are unusually low. For subsidiaries within a consolidated group, the discount rate (credit adjustment to the risk-free rate) should be specific to the entity that owns the long-lived asset to which the ARO is related and that is legally obligated for the asset retirement activity. However, the credit adjustment should take into consideration not only the credit standing of the entity that is legally obligated but also any other relevant facts, such as parent or brother/sister company guarantees of the entity's obligations and other methods of providing assurance that the entity's obligations will be paid, such as surety bonds, insurance policies, letters of credit, guarantees by other (unrelated) entities, or the establishment of trust funds or identification of other assets dedicated to satisfying the ARO. When determining the credit adjustment to the risk-free rate, nonpublic entities should use the same sources of information for determining discount rates that they use for mark-to-market calculations or determining the incremental borrowing rates for lease accounting or other purposes. Appropriate sources of this information for nonpublic entities might include financial institutions, other lenders, or comparable public companies.

4.4.2 Estimating Cash Flows and Applying an Expected Present Value Technique

The guidance in ASC 410-20-55-13 (reproduced above) includes consideration of a market risk premium when an expected present value technique is applied. Accordingly, when an entity performs a marketplace assessment of the cost of conducting required retirement activities, it must consider and determine a market risk premium that would be required for a third party to assume the retirement cost obligations — that is, the premium that a market participant would demand for bearing the uncertainty associated with the cash flows. If the entity is currently unable to obtain third-party quotes for the market risk premium for the specific retirement obligation (e.g., nuclear decommissioning), it should determine the premium for similar obligations (e.g., fossil plant dismantlement) and use that market risk premium as a minimum or increase that minimum to reflect the increased risk associated with the entity's specific retirement obligation. Predetermined percentage adjustments to retirement costs related to contingencies for unspecified additional costs, which may commonly be used in ARO cost studies, would not be considered an acceptable third-party market risk premium estimate.

Further, estimates for the demolition costs of a long-lived asset may include salvage credits for materials that can be sold. However, it is not appropriate for an entity to include estimated salvage credits when estimating expected cash flows to initially measure an ARO. ASC 410-20 applies only to "retirement" costs. Any estimated salvage value should be considered in connection with the calculation of depreciation of the related long-lived asset. The asset should be depreciated to reduce the net asset value so that it equals the estimated salvage value at the end of the asset's useful life.

In applying an expected present value technique, entities develop cash flow assumptions on the basis of the various costs that are necessary to achieve the required level of remediation, which will most likely take into consideration several possible outcomes in terms of total remediation costs required. They then multiply those outcomes by assigned probabilities, reflecting the estimated likelihood of occurrence of each potential outcome, to calculate the estimated expected cash flows, and this amount constitutes the (undiscounted) ARO under an expected present value technique. Entities need to use significant judgment in both estimating costs (cash flows) for various possible outcomes and assigning probabilities to the various outcomes. For a rate-regulated entity (such as a public utility), there may be a single estimate used to calculate the retirement costs that is based on a level of effort agreed to by a governing body, such as a state utility commission or the Federal Energy Regulatory Commission.

An entity's use of the probability weighting method on several possible cash flow scenarios in the application of an expected present value technique will almost certainly result in differences between actual asset retirement cash flows or their timing and the cash flows or timing incorporated into the initial measurement of an ARO. Further, incorporating third-party and marketplace assumptions into the estimate of ARO cash flows and the initial measurement of the ARO will most likely result in the recognition of gains upon the settlement of the ARO if the entity settles the obligation by using its own resources. These issues are addressed by the guidance in ASC 410-20 on subsequent recognition, subsequent measurement, and derecognition and are further discussed in Sections 4.5.1 through 4.5.3 below.

4.5 Subsequent Measurement of AROs and Asset Retirement Costs

---

ASC 410-20

Allocation of Asset Retirement Cost

35-1 A liability for an asset retirement obligation may be incurred over more than one reporting period if the events that create the obligation occur over more than one reporting period. Any incremental liability incurred in a subsequent reporting period shall be considered to be an additional layer of the original liability. Each layer shall be initially measured at fair value. For example, the liability for decommissioning a nuclear power plant is incurred as contamination occurs. Each period, as contamination increases, a separate layer shall be measured and recognized. Paragraph 410-20-30-1 provides guidance on using that technique.

35-2 An entity shall subsequently allocate that asset retirement cost to expense using a systematic and rational method over its useful life. Application of a systematic and rational allocation method does not preclude an entity from capitalizing an amount of asset retirement cost and allocating an equal amount to expense in the same accounting period. For example, assume an entity acquires a long-lived asset with an estimated life of 10 years. As that asset is operated, the entity incurs one-tenth of the liability for an asset retirement obligation each year. Application of a systematic and rational allocation method would not preclude that entity from capitalizing and then expensing one-tenth of the asset retirement costs each year.

35-3 In periods subsequent to initial measurement, an entity shall recognize period-to-period changes in the liability for an asset retirement obligation resulting from the following:

   a. The passage of time

   b. Revisions to either the timing or the amount of the original estimate of undiscounted cash flows.

35-4 An entity shall measure and incorporate changes due to the passage of time into the carrying amount of the liability before measuring changes resulting from a revision to either the timing or the amount of estimated cash flows.

35-5 An entity shall measure changes in the liability for an asset retirement obligation due to passage of time by applying an interest method of allocation to the amount of the liability at the beginning of the period. The interest rate used to measure that change shall be the credit-adjusted risk-free rate that existed when the liability, or portion thereof, was initially measured. That amount shall be recognized as an increase in the carrying amount of the liability and as an expense classified as accretion expense. Paragraph 835-20-15-7 states that accretion expense related to exit costs and asset retirement obligations shall not be considered to be interest cost for purposes of applying Subtopic 835-20.

35-6 The subsequent measurement provisions require an entity to identify undiscounted estimated cash flows associated with the initial measurement of a liability. Therefore, an entity that obtains an initial measurement of fair value from a market price or from a technique other than an expected present value technique must determine the undiscounted cash flows and estimated timing of those cash flows that are embodied in that fair value amount for purposes of applying the subsequent measurement provisions. Example 1 (see paragraph 410-20-55-31) provides an illustration of the subsequent measurement of a liability that is initially obtained from a market price. (See paragraph 410-20-25-14 for a discussion on conditional outcomes.)

35-7 Paragraph 410-20-25-14 explains how uncertainty surrounding conditional performance of a retirement obligation is factored into its measurement by assessing the likelihood that performance will be required. As the time for notification approaches, more information and a better perspective about the ultimate outcome will likely be obtained. Consequently, reassessment of the timing, amount, and probabilities associated with the expected cash flows may change the amount of the liability recognized. See paragraphs 410-20-55-18 through 55-19.

ASC 410-20 (continued)

Change in Estimate

35-8 Changes resulting from revisions to the timing or the amount of the original estimate of undiscounted cash flows shall be recognized as an increase or a decrease in the carrying amount of the liability for an asset retirement obligation and the related asset retirement cost capitalized as part of the carrying amount of the related long-lived asset. Upward revisions in the amount of undiscounted estimated cash flows shall be discounted using the current credit-adjusted risk-free rate. Downward revisions in the amount of undiscounted estimated cash flows shall be discounted using the credit-adjusted risk-free rate that existed when the original liability was recognized. If an entity cannot identify the prior period to which the downward revision relates, it may use a weighted-average credit-adjusted risk-free rate to discount the downward revision to estimated future cash flows. When asset retirement costs change as a result of a revision to estimated cash flows, an entity shall adjust the amount of asset retirement cost allocated to expense in the period of change if the change affects that period only or in the period of change and future periods if the change affects more than one period as required by paragraphs 250-10-45-17 through 45-20 for a change in estimate.

4.5.1 Capitalized Asset Retirement Costs

In subsequently accounting for the asset retirement cost capitalized as part of the tangible long-lived asset to which the ARO is related, an entity is required under ASC 410-20-35-2 to allocate that asset retirement cost to expense by using a systematic and rational method over the asset's useful life, which generally means that the asset retirement cost should be depreciated along with the related long-lived asset over the remaining economic useful life of the asset. However, this guidance does not preclude an entity from capitalizing an asset retirement cost and, depending on the facts and circumstances related to the ARO, allocating an equal amount to expense in the same accounting period.

The examples below illustrate the subsequent recognition of asset retirement costs as an expense over future periods.

Example 4-2

Company P owns several forests that are used in its production of paper. The company is under legal obligation to plant a tree for each tree it cuts down as part of retiring the asset (i.e., the forest). It plants a replacement tree concurrently with cutting down a tree.

The obligating event (cutting down trees) occurs in the current period regardless of whether the company plants the new trees immediately or waits until the end of the entire forest's useful life. If the company elects to plant the replacement tree immediately, the ARO will equal the current cost of planting the replacement tree. Since the company elects to plant the replacement tree in the same period in which it cuts down a tree, it is appropriate for the company to allocate an equal amount of the asset retirement cost to expense in the same accounting period.

Example 4-3

A limited-life partnership has been formed to mine minerals for the next 20 years. The partnership is legally responsible for the reclamation of the mine and the land upon termination of the partnership (i.e., in 20 years). In accordance with its legal obligation, the partnership has recorded an ARO and corresponding asset retirement cost for the present value (using 20 years) of the reclamation costs. The useful life of the mine is expected to extend for 50 years.

Expensing reclamation costs over the life of the partnership is appropriate in this situation. Before the guidance in ASC 410-20 became effective, industry practice for coal mines was to accrue reclamation costs over the life of the mine. In this case, the reclamation costs are required at the end of the partnership agreement. The useful life of the mine is expected to extend beyond the life of the partnership; however, since the partnership is required to perform the reclamation of the mine at the termination of the partnership agreement, the amortization period of the reclamation costs would be limited to the term of the agreement.

Connecting the Dots

In accordance with ASC 360-10-35-17 (which addresses accounting for the impairment of long-lived assets), an asset impairment loss is recorded only when the carrying amount of an asset is not recoverable and exceeds the asset's fair value. The carrying amount of a long-lived asset is not recoverable if it exceeds the sum of the undiscounted cash flows expected to result from the use and eventual disposition of the asset. An impairment loss should be measured as the amount by which the carrying amount of a long-lived asset exceeds its fair value. When performing the impairment calculation, an entity should include capitalized asset retirement costs in the evaluation of the asset. However, the estimated future cash flows related to the ARO should be excluded from (1) the undiscounted cash flows used to test the asset for recoverability and (2) the discounted cash flows used to measure the asset's fair value.

Further, in allocating the purchase price to a long-lived asset acquired and the related ARO assumed in a business combination transaction accounted for under ASC 805, an entity should measure and record both of the following:

- The ARO based on the fair value of the liability by using the credit-adjusted risk-free rate as of the acquisition date.

- The associated long-lived asset at fair value without considering any future cash outflows associated with the asset retirement activities and without adjustment to add the amount of the ARO.

4.5.2 Changes in an ARO Due to the Passage of Time

An entity is required to measure changes in an ARO due to the passage of time by using the interest method of allocation. The interest method of allocation requires an entity to use the credit-adjusted risk-free interest rate it used on the initial measurement date when it recognizes subsequent changes in the ARO. The amount is recognized as an increase (i.e., a credit) to the ARO, with the offsetting entry recorded in the income statement. The amount recorded in the income statement must be classified as an operating item and cannot be classified as interest expense. ASC 410-20-35-5 refers to this expense as accretion expense.

To calculate the accretion expense, an entity multiplies the ARO balance at the beginning of the period by the credit-adjusted risk-free rate that existed when the ARO was initially recognized. If an ARO is to be adjusted for both the passage of time and a revision of the estimated cash flows, the accretion expense due to the passage of time must be recognized first.

4.5.3 Changes in the Timing or Amount of Expected Cash Flows

When there is a change in the estimated timing or amount of expected cash flows of the retirement activity, the carrying amount of the liability should be adjusted either upward (as an increase in the ARO) or downward (as a decrease in the ARO), with the offset recorded as an increase or decrease in the related capitalized asset retirement cost. To calculate changes in the estimated timing or amount of expected cash flows that result in upward revisions to an ARO, an entity should use its then-current credit-adjusted risk-free interest rate. That is, the credit-adjusted risk-free rate in effect when the change occurs would be used to discount the revised estimate of the incremental expected cash flows of the retirement activity. However, if a change in the estimated timing or amount of expected cash flows results in a downward revision of an ARO, an entity should discount the undiscounted revised estimate of expected cash flows by using the credit-adjusted risk-free rate that was in effect on the date of initial measurement and recognition of the original ARO. The example below illustrates this concept.

Example 4-4

Assume that the undiscounted cost to perform a retirement activity 10 years from now is $100 and that the current credit-adjusted discount rate is 5 percent. The present value of the ARO would be accreted at 5 percent per year until year 10. In year 4, on the basis of updated information, the undiscounted cost to perform the retirement activity has increased by $5. The present value of the $5 would become a new cost layer that would be accreted at the then-current credit-adjusted discount rate (i.e., the credit-adjusted discount rate in year 4) until year 10.

When an entity is unable to identify the appropriate prior period to which downward adjustments of an ARO are related, it would be appropriate for that entity to use a weighted-average credit-adjusted risk-free rate to discount the revised estimated expected cash flows.

 Connecting the Dots

There is no explicit guidance in ASC 410-20 on the frequency with which an ARO should be reassessed to determine whether there have been changes in the estimated amount or timing of cash flows. In the absence of specific guidance, an entity should evaluate whether there are any indicators that would suggest that a change in the estimate of the ARO is necessary. Events or changes in circumstances that may indicate a need for reassessment include the following:

- A change in the law, regulation, or contract giving rise to the ARO that results in a change to either the timing of settlement or the expected retirement costs.

- A change in management's intended use of the asset, including a change in plans for maintaining the asset to extend its useful life or to abandon the asset earlier than previously expected.

- Advancements in technology that result in new methods of settlement or changes to existing methods of settlement.

- A change in economic assumptions, such as inflation rates.

An entity should analyze its specific facts and circumstances to determine whether the estimate of the ARO needs to be reassessed.

There may be situations in which the reduction of an ARO due to a revision of the original estimate of the timing or amount of the obligation exceeds the remaining associated unamortized asset retirement cost. In these circumstances, questions may arise about whether the difference should be recorded as a credit to the income statement or as a reduction of the carrying value of the related asset. The accounting will depend on whether the asset retirement cost and the related asset are viewed as a single asset or two discrete assets.

ASC 410-20-25-5 states, in part:

> Upon initial recognition of a liability for an asset retirement obligation, an entity shall capitalize an asset retirement cost by increasing the carrying amount of the related long-lived asset by the same amount as the liability.

ASC 410-20-35-2 states, in part:

> An entity shall subsequently allocate that asset retirement cost to expense using a systematic and rational method over its useful life.

ASC 410-20-25-5 appears to support a single-asset approach; however, ASC 410-20-35-2 could be interpreted to support a two-asset approach. If the asset retirement cost and related asset are viewed as a single asset, any downward adjustment of an ARO in excess of the related asset retirement cost should be recorded as a reduction of the carrying value of the related asset (although we believe that if the downward adjustment of the ARO results in a reduction of the carrying amount of the single asset to below zero, any excess should be recorded as a credit to the income statement). If the two-asset approach is applied, the downward adjustment of an ARO in excess of the asset retirement cost should be recorded as a credit to the income statement.

Connecting the Dots

We believe that the single-asset approach is preferable to the two-asset approach since it appears to be the one intended by the FASB given the following excerpt from paragraph B42 of the Background Information and Basis for Conclusions of FASB Statement 143:

> The Board believes that asset retirement costs are integral to or are a prerequisite for operating the long-lived asset and noted that current accounting practice includes in the historical-cost basis of an asset all costs that are necessary to prepare the asset for its intended use. Capitalized asset retirement costs are not a separate asset because there is no specific and separate future economic benefit that results from those costs. In other words, the future economic benefit of those costs lies in the productive asset that is used in the entity's operations.

Further, ASC 410-20-55-20 states:

> Revisions to the asset retirement obligation result in adjustments of capitalized asset retirement costs and will affect subsequent depreciation of the related asset. Such adjustments are depreciated on a prospective basis.

As previously noted, since an ARO is required to be initially measured at fair value incorporating marketplace assumptions, differences between estimated future costs used in the measurement of the fair value of an entity's ARO and actual expenditures incurred by that entity to settle the ARO may occur, resulting in a gain or loss. For example, a gain would most likely result when an entity elects to settle an ARO by using internal resources because the entity's internal costs are most likely less than the costs reflected in the fair value measurement of the ARO, which would be a function of the costs, profit margin, and market risk premium of a third party.

A gain or loss resulting from settlement of an ARO should be recognized in the period in which the asset retirement activities are performed. When asset retirement activities are performed over more than one reporting period, gains or losses should be recognized pro rata in accordance with the costs incurred during the period as compared with the total costs that the entity expects to incur to settle the ARO.

Example 4-5

Assume that (1) an entity recognized a liability for an ARO in the amount of $600,000 (based on a third-party estimate), (2) the entity expects to incur total costs of $400,000 to settle the ARO by using internal resources, and (3) the entity incurred $200,000 of costs during the current period. No costs were incurred by the entity before the current period. Ignoring the effects of discounting and other changes, the entity would reduce the ARO by $300,000 and recognize a gain of $100,000 during the current period.

Further assume that the remaining $200,000 of costs were incurred during the next reporting period. The entity would reduce the ARO by $300,000 (the ARO would be reduced to zero) and recognize a gain of $100,000 during the next reporting period.

It would be inappropriate to defer recognition of the entire gain or loss to the period in which the asset retirement activities are completed and the ARO is settled. Doing so would result in overstating or understating the ARO because it would not be representative of the amount that the entity would have to pay a third party to assume it.

This approach is supported by paragraph B41 of the Background Information and Basis for Conclusions of FASB Statement 143, which states, in part:

> The real issue is which period or periods should reflect the efficiencies of incurring lower costs than the costs that would be required by the market to settle the liability. The Board believes it is those periods in which the activities necessary to settle the liability are incurred.

4.6   Disclosure

ASC 410-20

50-1 An entity shall disclose all of the following information about its asset retirement obligations:

   a. A general description of the asset retirement obligations and the associated long-lived assets

   b. The fair value of assets that are legally restricted for purposes of settling asset retirement obligations

   c. A reconciliation of the beginning and ending aggregate carrying amount of asset retirement obligations showing separately the changes attributable to the following components, whenever there is a significant change in any of these components during the reporting period:

   1. Liabilities incurred in the current period

   2. Liabilities settled in the current period

   3. Accretion expense

   4. Revisions in estimated cash flows.

50-2 If the fair value of an asset retirement obligation cannot be reasonably estimated, that fact and the reasons therefor shall be disclosed.

ASC 410-20-50-1 and 50-2 provide disclosure requirements applicable to AROs. They require disclosure of (1) a general description of an entity's AROs and the associated long-lived assets and (2) the fair value of any assets legally restricted for purposes of settling AROs. In addition, they require tabular reconciliation of the beginning and ending aggregate carrying amount of AROs, showing separately changes attributable to new liabilities incurred, liabilities settled, accretion expense, and revisions in estimated cash flows, whenever there is a significant change in any of these components during a reporting period. When an entity cannot reasonably estimate the fair value of an ARO, the entity is required to disclose that fact and the reasons why a reasonable estimate of the ARO's fair value cannot be made.

Note that ASC 820-10 disclosures apply only to assets and liabilities measured at fair value in periods after initial recognition. The disclosures required by ASC 820-10 do not apply to AROs because the subsequent measurements are not at fair value.

4.6.1   Special Considerations for Oil and Gas Producing Activities

ASC 932 does not address the treatment of AROs or the related asset retirement costs. In February 2004, the SEC's Division of Corporation Finance sent a letter (the "February 2004 letter") to registrants primarily engaged in the production of oil and gas requesting that all registrants with subsidiaries or operations engaged in the production of oil and gas consider the letter in the preparation of their filings with the SEC. The scope of the February 2004 letter is limited to disclosure requirements for oil and gas producers.

4.6.1.1 Disclosure of Capitalized Costs Related to Oil and Gas Producing Activities

As stated in the February 2004 letter, the SEC staff believes that (1) "the reported carrying value of oil and gas properties should include the related asset retirement costs and accumulated depreciation" and (2) "depletion and amortization should include the accumulated allocation of the asset retirement costs since the beginning of the respective property's productive life."

Paragraph B46 of the Background Information and Basis for Conclusions of FASB Statement 143 discusses the Board's conclusion about the capitalization of asset retirement costs, stating that "a requirement for capitalization of an asset retirement cost along with a requirement for the systematic and rational allocation of it to expense achieves the objectives of (a) obtaining a measure of cost that more closely reflects the entity's total investment in the asset and (b) permitting the allocation of that cost, or portions thereof, to expense in the periods in which the related asset is expected to provide benefits." As noted in the February 2004 letter, excluding net capitalized asset retirement costs from the capitalized costs disclosure essentially would result in a presentation of capitalized costs that is not reflective of the entity's total investment in the asset, which is contrary to one of the objectives of ASC 410-20.

4.6.1.2 Disclosure of Costs Incurred in Oil and Gas Property Acquisition, Exploration, and Development Activities

The SEC staff believes that an entity should include asset retirement costs in its "costs incurred" disclosure in the year in which the liability is incurred, not on a cash basis. In addition, ASC 410-20 requires an entity to recognize the asset retirement costs and liability in the period in which it incurs the legal obligation — through either (1) the acquisition or development of an asset or (2) normal operation of the asset. Further, as stated in the February 2004 letter, the "cost of an asset retirement obligation is not incurred when the asset is retired and the obligation is settled. Accordingly, an entity should disclose the costs associated with an asset retirement obligation in the period in which that obligation is incurred. That is, the Costs Incurred disclosures in a given period should include asset retirement costs capitalized during the year and any gains or losses recognized upon settlement of asset retirement obligations during the period."

ASC 932-235-50-18 requires an entity to disclose costs incurred during the year regardless of whether those costs are capitalized or charged to expense.

4.6.1.3 Disclosure of the Results of Operations for Oil and Gas Producing Activities

The February 2004 letter expresses the SEC staff's belief that the "accretion of the liability for an asset retirement obligation should be included in the Results of Operations disclosure either as a separate line item, if material, or included in the same line item as it is presented on the statement of operations."

ASC 410-20-35-5 and ASC 410-20-45-1 together indicate that the accretion expense resulting from recognition of the changes in the liability for an ARO due to the passage of time should be classified as an operating item in the statement of income. Therefore, as stated in the February 2004 letter, "the accretion expense related to oil and gas properties' asset retirement obligations should be included in the [ASC 932-235] Results of Operations disclosure."

4.6.1.4 Disclosure of a Standardized Measure of Discounted Future Net Cash Flows Related to Proved Oil and Gas Reserve Quantities

The FASB staff and SEC staff believe that an entity should include the cash flows related to the settlement of an ARO in its "standardized measure" disclosure.

Under ASC 932-235-50-30, an entity is required to disclose as of the end of the year a standardized measure of discounted future net cash flows related to its interests in both (1) "[p]roved oil and gas reserves" and (2) "[o]il and gas subject to purchase under long-term supply, purchase, or similar agreements and contracts." The February 2004 letter expresses the SEC staff's belief that "the requirement to disclose 'net cash flows' relating to an entity's interest in oil and gas reserves requires an entity to include the cash outflows associated with the settlement of an asset retirement obligation. Exclusion of the cash flows associated with a retirement obligation would be a departure from the required disclosure. However, an entity is not prohibited from disclosing the fact that cash flows associated with asset retirement obligations are included in its Standardized Measure disclosure as a point of emphasis."

Chapter 5 — Industry Considerations Related to Asset Retirement Obligations and Environmental Obligations

This chapter provides further background and guidance on AROs (and in some cases, environmental remediation liabilities) commonly encountered by companies in various industries as a result of the nature of their business operations. The discussion in this chapter may refer to accounting practices often observed for companies in these industries related to their AROs and environmental remediation liabilities. Refer to the detailed accounting discussions in Chapters 3 and 4 for guidance on the initial and subsequent recognition and measurement of environmental remediation liabilities and AROs.

5.1 Landfill Operation

The modern landfill dates back to the late 1930s, when the first engineered landfill began operation in Fresno, California. Modern landfilling includes the intentional excavation or "berming up" of an area with the intention of containing the waste. Waste is placed, compacted, and covered on a daily basis, and landfill construction includes the use of materials, both natural and man-made, employed to reduce environmental impact.

Beginning in 1976 with the passage of RCRA, the EPA was tasked with developing and implementing solid waste management standards for landfills with respect to both hazardous and nonhazardous waste streams. Much of RCRA's subsequent amendments and additional regulations focused on the initial siting, design, and operation of solid waste facilities. RCRA also introduced requirements for closure, postclosure monitoring, and corrective action related to environmental contamination resulting from the landfills. A landfill ARO is based in part on these RCRA closure, postclosure, and corrective action regulations, as discussed previously in Chapter 2.

5.1.1 Landfill Construction

Landfill permits commonly limit the final dimensions of landfills, and landfills typically are constructed in sections called cells. The cells themselves can vary from entire, nearly independent waste areas to overlapping continuations of the cell before (like slices of bread in a loaf). The construction of a landfill using these smaller substructures allows the landfill to be constructed on an as-needed basis, with cells being constructed and finished just before they are needed. In addition to the capital benefit of the staggered construction of demand cells, there are also operational and closure benefits.

Landfill cells are constructed typically through the excavation of an area, the placement of lower liners consisting of compacted soils and engineered liner materials, and the installation of a leachate collection system. Many industry participants believe that before the placement of waste in a landfill cell, an ARO may exist but only for the cost of removing the installed materials from the cell. These companies believe that the obligating event for the recognition of AROs related to a particular landfill cell at an operating landfill is the placement of waste in that landfill cell, which occurs in relatively small increments over time. As landfill cells are added to the footprint of the landfill and additional waste is placed in these cells, ARO layers may be added to account for the new obligations. The timing and cost associated with the closure or retirement of each new cell may require consideration of variables that are both dependent on and independent of the larger landfill closure schedule.

Once a landfill cell is constructed with its regulation-compliant lower liner, the cell will collect water that must then be managed. If this water has come in contact with waste, it is considered to be leachate, and some level of treatment may be required before a company can dispose of it. An overly large cell may increase the volume of water to be managed. During operation of the landfill, the water or leachate management costs are generally considered to be ongoing maintenance costs in accordance with ASC 410-20-15-3(h) and are not part of an ARO.

5.1.2 Landfill Closure

Closure at a landfill is a complex and multifaceted process since closure obligations can be applied at both the cell and total landfill level. Further complicating matters, some portions of cell closure can begin before other portions of the cell have received waste.

Closure consists of four main activities or design considerations: slope stabilization, covering (or capping) a landfill, drainage control, and landfill gas management. Closure normally begins when a total airspace capacity of a cell has been consumed and no further waste is to be placed in the cell. When closure of a cell or an entire landfill begins, the following actions take place:

Slope stabilization — This involves large-scale grading of the final waste surface. The surface is graded to create a slope that is capable of achieving drainage and is structurally stable.

Covering (or capping) a landfill — The specific components of a landfill cover can vary, and there may be multiple technically feasible approaches to meeting the EPA requirements for water infiltration. However, the EPA requires the cover or cap to be at least as impermeable as the lower liner of the landfill. This requirement can result in different cap designs across a portfolio of landfills based on age and original construction. Landfill cover requirements are typically detailed in the landfill permit.

Drainage control — In addition to the actual cover layer, the landfill cap will include surface water drainage structures, such as ditches and letdown structures, along with a perimeter water management system.

Landfill gas management — A system of collection pipes, vents, or flares (or any such items in combination) is installed to collect gases generated during the decomposition of waste. Systems are installed during cap installation and are plumbed at the completion of cap installation.

Complicating the closure process, slope stabilization and the first layers of the landfill cover can begin when any portion of the landfill cell is filled to final grades. The grading of compacted waste to final slope topography and the placement of an intermediate cover could be regarded as part of the final closure obligation. These early and incremental closure activities complicate the estimation of the retirement obligation for each cell and for the landfill in total. The placement of waste and the daily cover of that waste represent ongoing operational costs, whereas the larger-scale grading and placement of buffer or intermediate cover materials as a part of closure (grading) or to delay the immediate need for closure (intermediate cover) may not be regarded as operational costs. Costs of grading and intermediate cover that are not operational costs should be included in the measurement of the liability for the ARO even though the tasks themselves may occur well in advance of the normal closure activities.

Final closure, which includes the placement of the cap materials, can occur in multiple stages during the life of a landfill and well before the entire landfill or even an entire cell is ready for final closure. Accordingly, the activities and costs underlying the ARO may occur in phases over time and not as a single event at a single point in time. While the total area to be closed and the associated cost may be known and estimable, the staging of the landfill closure affects closure timing, which a company should consider in the expected cash flow scenarios and, therefore, when measuring the fair value of the liability for an ARO.

5.1.3   Postclosure Care

At the completion of closure activities, landfill operators are required to conduct postclosure care (PCC). PCC is necessary because landfills are quite literally living things, or at least made up of a diverse ecosystem of organisms that slowly break down the waste. In addition to normal settlement resulting from gravity and the compaction of waste, the biological processes occurring within the landfill can reduce the volume of waste, resulting in settlement and subsidence.

RCRA Subtitle D requires PCC to be conducted for 30 years, although 40 CFR Section 258.61(b) stipulates that the length of PCC can be adjusted on the basis of site conditions, reduced, or increased on the basis of the demonstration of protectiveness. When measuring an ARO for landfill closure, a company should generally consider a period of 30 years for PCC unless the site-specific permit stipulates otherwise.

Under 40 CFR Section 258.61(a), PCC requires the following:

- "Maintaining the integrity and effectiveness of any final cover, including making repairs to the cover as necessary to correct the effects of settlement, subsidence, erosion, or other events, and preventing run-on and run-off from eroding or otherwise damaging the final cover."

- "Maintaining and operating the leachate collection system in accordance with the requirements in [40 CFR Section] 258.40, if applicable. The Director of an approved State may allow the owner or operator to stop managing leachate if the owner or operator demonstrates that leachate no longer poses a threat to human health and the environment."

- "Monitoring the ground water in accordance with the requirements of subpart E of [40 CFR Part 258] and maintaining the ground-water monitoring system, if applicable."

- "Maintaining and operating the gas monitoring system in accordance with the requirements of [40 CFR Section] 258.23."

The site-specific permit for a landfill may specify additional terms for PCC that should be considered for each landfill unit. The biological breakdown of waste can result in the formation of landfill gas and the release of leachate, which comes from (1) the moisture in the waste, (2) precipitation into the landfill cell before closure, and (3) the infiltration of precipitation through the final cover. Leachate recovery volumes typically peak in the first few years after closure and decrease to a steady-state volume at some point before PCC is complete. The modeling of leachate generation is commonly used for estimating the annual treatment costs; however, since there may not be sufficient data available in the first few years of PCC for a company to estimate volumes or the decline curve for the remaining PCC period, care should be taken to update ARO cost estimates regularly on the basis of observed volumes. Similarly, the estimation of landfill gas generation is possible and can be extrapolated to allow a company to estimate the operating life of the gas management facilities, and care should therefore be taken to update the cash flow estimates underlying the ARO.

Leachate generation rates should be assessed annually for most landfills, and the leachate treatment costs included in the ARO should be reevaluated. Leachate generation can indicate other landfill closure health issues and can function as a barometer for future costs. Generation that does not decline could indicate issues with landfill cap construction, which may require repair at additional costs. Significant leachate generation may also extend the PCC period required to show stability and no further risk to human health and the environment.

As discussed above, closure for landfill cells may be staged and may not occur as a single event. This staged closure may affect the PCC period since the start of the 30 years of PCC for a cell may differ from the start of the PCC period for other cells or the landfill as a whole. Many state regulators require some type of closure verification to be submitted before they will consider closure to be complete. The acceptance of this closure verification should be used as the basis for beginning the PCC period. When certification of closure is not available, evidence should be sought to validate any assumption that PCC has begun for a particular cell or closure area. Since the groundwater monitoring network encapsulates the entire site and can rarely be isolated to any portion of the landfill, PCC for groundwater monitoring typically does not commence until the complete closure of the landfill. In addition, surface maintenance, security and site access, utilities, and administrative functions are commonly provided at an overall site level and may be required for the full PCC time frame after the final closure at the site.

5.1.4 Contingent Liability at a Solid Waste Facility

As discussed in Chapters 1 and 4, it is possible that liabilities arising at a solid waste facility are not within the scope of the guidance in ASC 410-20 on AROs but represent other contingent or environmental remediation liabilities within the scope of ASC 450 and ASC 410-30. See Chapter 1 for further discussion of the scope of ASC 410-20 and ASC 410-30.

As related to solid waste facilities, the type of environmental contamination incurred in the normal operation of the asset that would also be associated with the retirement of that asset would most likely include any site cleanup not specifically included in the operating permit but still required at closure. Examples of such site cleanup are:

- Cleanup, repair, or remediation of infrastructure or access roads and parking areas associated with the landfill.

- Remediation of soil and groundwater affected by a truck washing facility.

- Remediation of equipment maintenance facilities on-site.

- Remediation of storm water management impoundments on-site.

The above examples are remediation activities that are required only as a result of the normal operation of a landfill and only at the time of retirement of all or part of the facility. However, remediation that is required before or after the closure of the site may not be a result of the normal operation of the landfill, as in the following examples:

- Remediation of soil and groundwater affected by accidental discharges and spills on-site.

- Remediation of groundwater affected by a leaking landfill. While an argument could be made that leaks are a normal and expected event arising from historically constructed landfills, an environmental remediation liability may exist when (1) the leakage is beyond what is expected from the normal operation of the landfill and (2) remediation is required before retirement of the asset. For additional discussion, see Chapter 1.

5.2 Mining

Mining has occurred in some form since the beginning of civilization, and the methods of extracting the various commodities have not changed significantly since that time. Mining traditionally requires excavation either at surface or in the subsurface, with different retirement obligations associated with each. Solution or in situ leaching is also an extraction method common with soluble minerals and metals such as uranium, potash, and sodium chloride. While federal mining regulations do exist and are applicable on federally managed lands, most mining is regulated at the state and local levels. The AROs associated with mining activities are most commonly created as a result of permit requirements for the closure and reclamation of a mine at the end of permit life or operations.

The environmental impact and retirement obligations common to mining are divided into two categories on the basis of the operation of a mine: extraction phase and processing phase. While all mines have an extraction phase, not all mines will have on-site processing. The retirement obligations between the two phases are different, and the accounting considerations and common practices are also different.

5.2.1 Extraction Phase

As with most AROs, the specific requirements for retirement are typically contained in site-specific permits. In a manner similar to that of landfill permits, permits for mines may only outline the extent of operations and contain a general reference to a state or federal closure requirement. Commonly, we have observed that state permits require only that at some point immediately (6–12 months) before ceasing operations, a mine should submit a closure plan. While this closure plan provides more specifics to the closure, it does not create the retirement obligation. That is, a retirement obligation exists before a closure plan is developed, and the ARO is triggered by the excavation and the mine's operational activities, the terms of the related permits, and applicable state and federal statutes. The closure plan provides detail regarding how specifically the mine will be reclaimed. A mine operator may know the reclamation methods to be used and have a general understanding and estimate of the extent of such activities and related costs before it develops a closure plan.

The reclamation of a surface mine is often driven by the need to make the area safe and stable. This is particularly true for highwall mines. Rarely is the complete backfilling of a mine required or feasible. However, backfill and grading may be required to make slopes sustainable, to limit erosion or surface water impacts, and to prevent access. Revegetation and the removal of infrastructure may also be required. The activities common in mine reclamation may be straightforward, but the estimation and maintenance of a mine ARO are anything but. As in the case of landfills, the many variables associated with the timing and extent of reclamation activities could make the initial and subsequent measurement of an ARO challenging.

5.2.2 Processing Phase

Many minerals and metals require processing after they are extracted for the high-value commodities from the ore to be concentrated or further extracted. Processing can include milling, leaching, smelting, concentration and flotation, and electrowinning. At some mines, ore processing activities occur at the mine site, and these activities may be included in the mining permit or another operating permit. In addition to environmental regulations related to the operation of the processing facility, some operating permits have extensive retirement obligations.

The mining method of processing through leaching is commonly used for the extraction of metals such as copper and gold. Leaching at a commercial mine can occupy hundreds of acres, creating both significant retirement obligations and potential environmental remediation liabilities. The leaching of metals through heap leaching involves the loose piling of extracted and crushed ore over a plastic-lined pad area (the "heap leach pad"). The closure of a heap leach pad requires the complete removal of spent ore, berms, pad liners, and all associated plumbing and processing equipment. In addition, if any ponds were created for the processing, these ponds must be drained, with all liquids treated and disposed of and all liners removed.

The removal of liners may result in the identification of soil contamination beneath the heap leach pad due to liner failures. This type of impact could meet the definition of contamination resulting from the normal operation of the asset when treatment is required at retirement and therefore part of the ARO. However, the failure of a berm on a heap leach pad, resulting in the sudden loss of process water and contamination of surrounding soils, could be an example of contamination not associated with normal operation, potentially creating an environmental remediation liability within the scope of ASC 410-30. While the cost of decommissioning and reclaiming an area used for heap leach processing may be estimable since the surface area and decommissioning activities required are known, the cost of any additional remediation may not be estimable before retirement.

In addition to the retirement obligations addressed above, the operation of a mine and particularly the operation of on-site ore processing can result in environmental contamination that is not associated with the normal operation and ultimate retirement of the processing facility. For example, consider acid rock drainage, a naturally occurring process in which rocks high in sulfide minerals are disturbed and exposed to rainfall and surface waters. The exposure of the sulfide minerals to air and water can result in the oxidation of the minerals and the formation of a low-pH acidic solution. When this chemical process occurs at a mine, either active or abandoned, it is called acid mine drainage (AMD). At an active mine, operational processes and controls may be in place to control the formation of AMD and to limit the off-site migration or flow of low-pH water. When these processes and controls fail, it is possible for contamination to leave the site, resulting in the need for remediation. Since this type of contamination may not be from the normal operation of the mine or is not associated with the retirement of the asset, the related remediation obligation may not be regarded as an ARO but may need to be treated as an environmental obligation that should be accounted for under ASC 410-30.

5.3 Power and Utilities — Nuclear

The NRC defines decommissioning as permanently removing a nuclear facility from service and reducing radioactive material on the licensed site to levels that permit termination of the NRC license. Legal obligations associated with the decommissioning of a nuclear power plant generally are within the scope of ASC 410-20.

5.3.1 Nuclear Power Plant Decommissioning

Decommissioning involves removing the spent fuel (i.e., the fuel that has been in the reactor vessel), dismantling any systems or components containing activated material (such as the reactor vessel and primary loop), and cleaning up or dismantling contaminated materials from the facility. All activated materials generally have to be removed from the site and shipped to a waste processing, storage, or disposal facility.

The legal obligation associated with the decommissioning of a nuclear power plant arises from the regulations established by the NRC. Before a nuclear power plant begins operations, the NRC requires the licensee to establish or obtain a financial mechanism, such as a trust fund or a guarantee from its parent company, to ensure that there will be sufficient money to cover the cost for the ultimate decommissioning of the facility. The minimum decommissioning funding required by the NRC reflects only the efforts necessary to terminate the NRC license, which is commonly known as the "Part 50 license."[1] This license is not terminated until the licensee has completed all activities included in the approved license termination plan (LTP). Other activities related to facility deactivation and site closure, including operation of the spent fuel storage pool, construction and operation of an independent spent fuel storage installation (ISFSI), demolition of decontaminated structures, and site restoration activities after residual radioactivity has been removed, are not included in the NRC definition of decommissioning. However, costs for the completion of these activities are typically included in the decommissioning cost estimate because there may be a legal obligation imposed by the state or local government, or both, for ultimate release of the property.

Under 10 CFR Section 50.75, each nuclear power plant licensee must report to the NRC every two years the status of its decommissioning fund for each reactor or share of a reactor that it owns. At or about five years before the projected end of operations, each power reactor licensee must submit to the NRC a preliminary decommissioning cost estimate that includes an up-to-date assessment of the major factors that could affect the cost of decommissioning the reactor.

In addition, 10 CFR Section 50.82 requires a nuclear power plant licensee to submit a post-shutdown activities report (PSDAR) to the NRC, as well as a copy to the affected state(s), before or within two years after permanent cessation of operations. The PSDAR must contain the following:

- A description of the planned decommissioning activities.
- A schedule for the accomplishment of significant milestones.
- Documentation that environmental impacts associated with site-specific decommissioning activities have been considered in previously approved environmental impact statements.
- A site-specific decommissioning cost estimate, including the projected cost of managing irradiated fuel.

Under 10 CFR Section 50.82, a nuclear power plant licensee is also required to submit an LTP at least two years before its license is terminated. The LTP must include the following:

- A site characterization.
- Identification of remaining dismantlement activities.
- Plans for site remediation.
- Detailed plans for the final survey of residual contamination at the site.
- A description of the end use of the site, if restricted.
- An updated site-specific estimate of remaining decommissioning costs.
- A supplement to the environmental report.

---

[1] The term "Part 50 license" refers to 10 CFR Part 50, the citation to the corresponding regulations in the *Code of Federal Regulations*.

5.3.2 Nuclear Plant Decommissioning Alternatives

The nuclear decommissioning cost estimate must reflect the type of decommissioning alternative selected. In accordance with 10 CFR Parts 30, 40, 50, 51, 70, and 72, a nuclear power plant licensee may choose from three decommissioning alternatives: DECON, SAFSTOR, or ENTOMB. These alternatives are summarized in the diagram below.

DECON	Under DECON (immediate dismantling), soon after the nuclear facility closes, equipment, structures, and portions of the facility containing radioactive contaminants are removed or decontaminated to a level that permits release of the property and termination of the NRC license.
SAFSTOR	Under SAFSTOR (deferred dismantling), a nuclear facility is maintained and monitored in a condition that allows the radioactivity to decay; afterward, the plant is dismantled and the property decontaminated. Spent fuel is removed from the spent fuel pools (wet storage) and placed into dry storage (ISFSI).
ENTOMB	Under ENTOMB, radioactive contaminants are permanently encased on-site in structurally sound material such as concrete. The facility is maintained and monitored until the radioactivity decays to a level that permits restricted release of the property. According to the information available on the NRC's Web site at this time, none of the NRC-licensed facilities currently undergoing decommissioning have requested ENTOMB.

Decommissioning must be completed within 60 years of the plant's cessation of operations. A time beyond that would be considered only when necessary to protect public health and safety in accordance with NRC regulations.

It has been observed in industry that licensees often change their decommissioning alternative selection during the life of the plant. For example, a licensee that originally anticipated decommissioning a power plant under the DECON alternative may change this decision and select SAFSTOR on the basis of external factors. If the decommissioning alternative is changed, the decommissioning cost estimate must be revised accordingly.

5.3.3 High-Level Radioactive Waste

Highly radioactive byproducts of the reactions that occur inside nuclear reactors are called high-level radioactive waste. There are two types of high-level radioactive waste: (1) spent fuel when it is accepted for disposal and (2) waste materials remaining after spent fuel is reprocessed. High-level radioactive waste must be handled and stored with care because of its highly radioactive fission products.

The only way that radioactive waste can become harmless is through decay. However, it can take hundreds of thousands of years for high-level radioactive waste to fully decay. For that reason, high-level radioactive waste must be stored and finally disposed of in a way that provides the public with adequate protection for a very long time.

In 1982, Congress passed the Nuclear Waste Policy Act, assigning the federal government's long-standing responsibility for disposal of spent nuclear fuel created by commercial nuclear generating plants to the U.S. Department of Energy (DOE). The DOE was to begin accepting spent fuel by January 31, 1998; however, no progress has been made to date in the removal of spent fuel from commercial generating sites. In January 2013, the DOE issued the document *Strategy for the Management and Disposal of Used Nuclear Fuel and High-Level Radioactive Waste* (the "January 2013 document"). In its January 2013 document, the DOE stated that "[w]ith the appropriate authorizations from Congress, the Administration currently plans to implement a program over the next 10 years that . . . [a]dvances toward the siting and licensing of a larger interim storage facility to be available by 2025 that will have sufficient capacity to provide flexibility in the waste management system and allows for acceptance of enough used nuclear fuel to reduce expected government liabilities."

Completion of the decommissioning process is dependent on the DOE's ability to remove spent fuel from the site in a timely manner. As a result of the DOE's current inability to accept the spent fuel, commercial generating sites have been storing their high-level radioactive waste in the ISFSI, which is typically located on the same property as the nuclear reactor. Costs associated with the long-term storage of the spent fuel are typically included in the decommissioning estimate. Costs for storage include operation and maintenance of the ISFSI and security as required under NRC regulations.

It is important to consider the uncertainties associated with both the requirements related to the storage of spent nuclear fuel and the timing and ultimate disposal of spent fuel, as well as how those uncertainties may affect ARO cost estimates. Three approaches have been observed in industry with respect to the estimation of when the DOE will be able to accept spent fuel from a nuclear power plant:

1. The DOE will not be able to accept spent fuel, and the material will remain on-site indefinitely.

2. The DOE will accept the spent fuel at a later time based on an adjustment to the pickup date provided in the DOE's July 2004 *Acceptance Priority Ranking & Annual Capacity Report*, taking into account the 2025 spent fuel pickup start date provided in the DOE's January 2013 document.

3. An approach similar to that in (2) above, but with a spent fuel pickup start date later than 2025 based on professional judgment.

In addition, many of the commercial generators have entered into settlement agreements with the DOE to obtain reimbursement from the DOE for costs related to spent fuel that were incurred as a result of the DOE's delay in taking possession of spent fuel. In practice, we have observed several instances in which nuclear power generators obtained (1) reimbursements from the federal government or state regulatory agencies for operations and maintenance costs or (2) other monetary damages associated with the federal government's failure to begin removing spent nuclear fuel and other radioactive waste from former nuclear reactor sites.

5.4 Power and Utilities — Non-Nuclear

The power and utilities (P&U) industry includes many technologies for the generation of electricity, and companies in this industry are likely to have multiple AROs associated with the array of assets required for the generation and delivery of electricity. Common P&U generation methods and corresponding potential AROs include the following:

P&U Generation Method	Potential ARO
Coal-fired generation	Coal ash impoundments
Manufactured gas plants	Storage tanks, impoundments, and vaults
Solar	Solar array and associated structures
Wind	Turbines

In addition, as noted in Chapter 4, the common utility pole used in the distribution of electric power (and telecommunications) may also be subject to unique disposal requirements, creating an ARO for the disposal of the utility pole once the pole is extracted and removed from service.

5.4.1 Coal Ash Impoundments

The burning of coal results in the generation of coal combustion residuals commonly called coal ash. Depending on the technology used to handle air emissions created during the burning of coal, ash is generated in either a dry or wet form, to be handled either on-site or off-site. When managed off-site, the ash generated leaves the site without long-term on-site storage. At facilities where the ash is retained on-site, impoundments are commonly used to contain the waste material. Coal ash impoundments, also known as ash landfills, coal ash ponds, and flue gas disposal ponds, were not universally regulated in the United States until December 19, 2014. Before that date, the operation and closure of these impoundments were regulated at the state level if they were regulated at all. That is, in some states, the management of coal ash was not regulated, and no obligation related to the handling and retirement of ash impoundments previously existed. On December 19, 2014, after more than six years of regulatory development, the EPA released the Disposal of Coal Combustion Residuals From Electric Utilities final rule (the "CCR rule"). The rule was later published in the *Federal Register*, taking effect on April 17, 2015.

The CCR rule, while complicated in how it is enforced, effectively created a single standard for the operation and closure of impoundments containing coal ash across the United States. In states where no regulation existed before, the CCR rule created a retirement obligation. However, in states that previously regulated the closure of these impoundments, the CCR rule either reinforced or amended the existing state requirements. As a result, the recognition and measurement of retirement obligations created by the CCR rule have given rise to diversity and complexity in practice, particularly for utilities operating in many states.

While the CCR rule is fairly straightforward, the initial recognition of an ARO for a long-lived asset that is already well into its estimated life is more complicated. As previously discussed in Chapter 4, ASC 410-20-25-4 requires an entity to recognize the fair value of an ARO in the period in which the liability is incurred if a reasonable estimate of the fair value of the liability can be made. Making a reasonable estimate of the obligation associated with closing an often old and complex ash impoundment proved challenging immediately after the CCR rule became law. Estimating the retirement or closure costs often required the estimation of ash volumes already within the impoundments, in some situations with very little information available about the original design or capacity of the impoundment. Many affected companies initially measured and recorded AROs on the basis of the best information then available and subsequently refined their estimates each period as additional information was obtained through studies and investigations. The immediate lack of availability of complete information generally did not prevent the recognition of some portion of the liability.

Because of the CCR rule, many entities began accounting for AROs associated with coal ash impoundments for the first time. Consequently, the application of the accounting guidance in ASC 410-20 to these AROs proved challenging. Challenges include, but are not limited to, the following:

- Inclusion of operational costs before closure (e.g., groundwater monitoring, maintenance) in the measurement of the ARO.
- Failure to include long-term PCC activities after closure.
- Estimates using internal cost without proper consideration of fair value concepts (e.g., profit margin, risk premiums).
- Basic estimate lacking due diligence and consideration of leading industry practices.

Assumptions included in an ARO estimate should be well supported, and consideration should be given to the expertise of those persons who develop ARO estimates. Assistance from external subject matter experts may be required.

Connecting the Dots
Accounting for New AROs

As additional information becomes available, entities should continually reassess AROs, particularly when accounting for new AROs created by newly enacted laws or regulations. Chapter 4 provides additional guidance on the accounting for changes to an ARO that result from changes in the timing or amount of expected cash flows. Further, in these circumstances, entities should ensure that those responsible for the development of asset retirement/closure cost estimates are familiar with the accounting guidance, or that there is extensive coordination between operational personnel, subject matter experts, and finance/accounting personnel with expertise in the requirements of ASC 410-20 when developing the cost estimates and other assumptions that underlie an ARO.

Consistency of ARO Cost Estimates

A company may be required, in accordance with the terms of an operating permit or otherwise, to obtain certain forms of financial assurance associated with an ARO to guarantee the funding needed to satisfy the ARO in the event of the company's insolvency. Under ASC 410-20-35-9, methods of providing assurance include surety bonds, insurance policies, letters of credit, and establishment of trust funds or identification of other assets dedicated to satisfying an ARO.

Obtaining financial assurance typically requires a company to submit cost estimates associated with satisfying its ARO. An estimate developed for assurance or insurance purposes may include or exclude costs that should be excluded from or included in the measurement of an ARO under ASC 410-20, or it may be based on assumptions regarding timing or method of settlement that are inconsistent with the requirements of ASC 410-20. However, a company should evaluate the consistency of cost estimates made for assurance or insurance purposes when measuring the fair value of an ARO under the guidance in ASC 410-20 to understand the reasons for any significant differences.

5.4.2 Manufactured Gas Plants

Manufactured gas plants (MGPs) in the United States date back to the early 19th century and were in operation as late as the mid-1970s. The manufacturing of synthetic gas (Syngas) was necessary because of the limited availability of natural gas and the difficulty of transporting it. The chemical process, while relatively simple, resulted in significant amounts of residual waste. The waste products, which are persistent, still contaminate many former MGP sites and are the basis for many environmental remediation liabilities. The contamination from former MGP operations may have continued over decades, and in many cases, this contamination has remained unremediated. The result is often contamination spread across a site horizontally, with vertical distribution from near the surface to well below groundwater and into bedrock.

In terms of accounting for MGP liabilities, there is no clear industry consensus on whether the remediation costs should be treated as AROs under ASC 410-20 or as environmental remediation liabilities under ASC 410-30. When it can be clearly shown that the regulatory remediation obligations can be delayed (to a point that they can be reasonably estimated), it may be appropriate to treat the liabilities as AROs. When the regulatory remediation obligations cannot be further delayed, treatment as environmental remediation liabilities may be appropriate.

5.5   Asbestos

Asbestos is a group of naturally occurring minerals with thin fibrous crystals that can be released when disturbed. Asbestos fibers have been linked to many medical conditions and as a result have been regulated in some manner for the past 50 years. While regulations in the United States have not completely banned the use of asbestos, there are various federal and state regulations related to the disposal of asbestos-containing material (ACM). The regulation of the disposal of ACM results in a retirement obligation for ACM.

ACM has insulating and strengthening characteristics and is commonly found in building insulation, pipe wrap, flooring and roofing, and gaskets. It is most often encountered during building demolition and remodeling or repair. Because many states regulate only the disposal of ACM, the settlement date for the obligation to address the ACM may be uncertain and will depend on when the asset containing the ACM is disposed of (which may be subject to significant management discretion).

ASC 410-20-55-57 through 55-62 address the availability of sufficient information and the ability to reasonably estimate the fair value of an ARO related to the removal and disposal of asbestos. When ACM is known to exist, a market participant would presumably consider the cost of addressing the liability in any purchase regardless of settlement date. As with other AROs, uncertainty of timing should not otherwise prevent the recognition of an ARO, and the uncertainty should be incorporated in the fair value measurement.

5.6   Oil and Gas

The oil and gas industry is subject to retirement obligations across the entire industry value chain, from the upstream extraction of hydrocarbons to the downstream processing and ultimately the retail distribution of refined products. Retirement obligations in the industry include those associated with the following systems and facilities:

- Upstream:
  - Oil wells.
  - Saltwater disposal wells.
  - Well pads — including tank batteries, ponds, and other improvements.
- Midstream:
  - Gathering systems.
  - Transmission lines.
  - Pressurization systems.
- Downstream:
  - Refineries.
  - Liquefied natural gas terminals.
  - Shipping terminals.
- Retail:
  - Underground storage tanks.
  - Aboveground storage tanks.

- Offshore:
  - Pipelines.
  - Platforms.
  - Wells.

With the assets above, regulations or lease agreements may require the abandonment in place or removal of the structure at the end of the useful life of the asset. Some midstream (pipeline) assets are considered to operate in perpetuity on the basis of the expectation of repair and maintenance rather than removal and retirement. On the retail side, underground storage tanks must be removed, and some level of soil remediation is often required as a result of unintentional leaks. Because of complexities of working offshore along with increased regulatory scrutiny, the cost of offshore decommissioning is often significantly higher than that of similar onshore activities.

Appendix A — Differences Between U.S. GAAP and IFRS Standards

Environmental Remediation Liabilities

Under U.S. GAAP, ASC 410-30 provides accounting guidance on environmental remediation liabilities. The guidance in ASC 410-30 is generally based on the framework outlined in ASC 450-20.

Under IFRS® Standards, there is no standard that specifically addresses accounting for environmental remediation liabilities. Rather, entities applying IFRS Standards account for environmental remediation liabilities in accordance with IAS 37. Under IFRS Standards, IAS 37 is the primary source of guidance on contingencies.

There are differences between ASC 450-20 and IAS 37, including, but not limited to, those in the table below.

Subject	U.S. GAAP	IFRS Standards
Scope	ASC 450 applies to asset impairments.	IAS 37 does not apply to asset impairments.
Terminology	Three categories: • Estimated loss accrued for a loss contingency (i.e., a contingent loss that is recognized as a liability). • Contingent loss that is not recognized as a liability. • Contingent gain.	Three categories: • Provision. • Contingent liability. • Contingent asset.
Recognition of contingent losses/provisions	One of the conditions for loss accrual is that it is probable that (1) an asset has been impaired or (2) a liability has been incurred. "Probable" is defined as likely, which is a higher threshold than "more likely than not."	One of the conditions for recognizing a provision (as a liability) is that it is probable that an outflow of resources will be required to settle the obligation. "Probable" is defined as more likely than not.
Measurement of contingent losses/provisions — range of estimates	If no amount in the range is more likely than any other amount in the range, the minimum amount in the range is used to measure the amount to be accrued for a loss contingency.	If no amount in the range is more likely than any other amount in the range, the midpoint of the range is used to measure the liability.
Measurement of contingent losses/provisions — discounting	Discounting is permitted only when the timing of related cash flows is fixed or reliably determinable.	Discounting is required if the effect of discounting is material.

103

(Table continued)

Subject	U.S. GAAP	IFRS Standards
Recoveries of contingent losses (reimbursements)	Expected reimbursements related to the recovery of contingent losses are recognized when recovery is deemed probable.	Expected reimbursement by other parties is recognized only when it is virtually certain that the reimbursement will be received.
Onerous contracts	Losses on firmly committed onerous contracts are usually not recognized.	If an entity has a contract that is onerous, the present obligation under the contract should be recognized as a liability.
Disclosure of prejudicial information	Exemptions from disclosure of information that may be prejudicial to an entity are not permitted.	In extremely rare cases, if disclosure of certain information could prejudice the position of the entity in a dispute with other parties, that information does not need to be disclosed. However, the entity must disclose the nature of the dispute, along with the reason why the information has not been disclosed.
Gain contingencies (U.S. GAAP) versus contingent assets (IFRS Standards)	When realization of a gain contingency is assured beyond a reasonable doubt, recognition is appropriate.	When realization of a contingent asset is virtually certain, recognition is appropriate.

Asset Retirement Obligations

Under U.S. GAAP, ASC 410-20 is the primary source of guidance on accounting for obligations associated with the retirement of tangible long-lived assets.

Under IFRS Standards, IAS 16 provides guidance on accounting for costs of dismantling and removing property, plant, and equipment, and restoring the site on which it was located when an item is acquired or as a consequence of using the item during a particular period other than to produce inventory. In addition, IAS 37 (see the table above for a summary of certain guidance in IAS 37, including the standard's initial recognition guidance) addresses the measurement of decommissioning, restoration, and similar liabilities, and IFRIC Interpretation 1 addresses how to account for changes in existing decommissioning, restoration, and similar liabilities.

The table below summarizes the key differences between U.S. GAAP and IFRS Standards in accounting for obligations associated with the retirement of tangible long-lived assets.

Subject	U.S. GAAP	IFRS Standards
Initial measurement of an ARO	The fair value of an ARO liability is recognized in the period it is incurred if a reasonable estimate of fair value can be made. When a present value technique is used to estimate the liability, the discount rate will be a risk-free interest rate adjusted for the effect of the entity's credit standing. Probability is factored into the measurement of an ARO but is not factored into the recognition of an ARO.	ARO liability is measured as the best estimate of the expenditure to settle the obligation or to transfer the obligation to a third party as of the balance sheet date. When a present value technique is used to estimate the liability, the discount rate will be a pretax rate that reflects current market assessments of the time value of money and the risks specific to the liability.

(Table continued)

Subject	U.S. GAAP	IFRS Standards
Asset recognition from an ARO	Upon initial recognition of a liability as an ARO, an entity increases the related long-lived asset by the same amount.	Property, plant, and equipment include the initial estimate of the ARO unless it is incurred during a period in which the property was used to produce inventory, in which case the ARO would be added to the carrying amount of the inventory.
Subsequent measurement of an ARO	Period-to-period revisions to either the timing or amount of the original estimate of undiscounted cash flows are treated as separate layers of the obligation. An entity should discount upward revisions by using the current credit-adjusted risk-free rate, and it should discount downward revisions by using the original credit-adjusted risk-free rate.	The ARO should be adjusted for changes in the estimate of expected undiscounted cash flows or discount rate as of each balance sheet date. An entity should remeasure the entire obligation by using an updated discount rate that reflects current market conditions as of the balance sheet date.

Appendix B — Environmental Literature

The sources listed below, from which much of the material in Chapters 2 and 5 of this Roadmap is adapted, provide additional information related to environmental obligations and AROs.

Section	Section Title	Source	URL
2.1	Environmental Regulations — Federal		
2.1.1	The CAA	EPA, "Clean Air Act Requirements and History"	https://www.epa.gov/clean-air-act-overview/clean-air-act-requirements-and-history
		EPA, "1990 Clean Air Act Amendment Summary: Introduction"	https://www.epa.gov/clean-air-act-overview/1990-clean-air-act-amendment-summary
		EPA, "1990 Clean Air Act Amendment Summary: Title III: Air Toxics"	https://www.epa.gov/clean-air-act-overview/1990-clean-air-act-amendment-summary-title-iii
		EPA, "Clean Air Act Amendment Summary: Title V: Permits"	https://www.epa.gov/clean-air-act-overview/1990-clean-air-act-amendment-summary-title-v
		EPA, "Setting Emissions Standards Based on Technology Performance"	https://www.epa.gov/clean-air-act-overview/setting-emissions-standards-based-technology-performance
		EPA, "Information Regarding Implementation of the Emission Trading Program Pursuant to 45 CSR28, 'Air Pollutant Emissions Banking and Trading'"	https://www.epa.gov/title-v-operating-permits/information-regarding-implementation-emission-trading-program-pursuant-45
		EPA, "Clean Air Markets — Allowance Markets: Overview"	https://www.epa.gov/airmarkets/clean-air-markets-allowance-markets
2.1.2	The CWA	EPA, "Summary of the Clean Water Act"	https://www.epa.gov/laws-regulations/summary-clean-water-act
		Transportation Environmental Resource Center, "Clean Water Act (CWA): Industrial Wastewater"	http://www.tercenter.org/regulations/cwa.cfm
2.1.3	The TSCA	EPA, "Summary of the Toxic Substances Control Act"	https://www.epa.gov/laws-regulations/summary-toxic-substances-control-act

(Table continued)

Section	Section Title	Source	URL
2.1.3	The TSCA	EPA Office of Research and Development (ORD), *Children's Environmental Health Research Roadmap*	https://nepis.epa.gov/Exe/ZyPDF.cgi/P100NGB5.PDF?Dockey=P100NGB5.pdf
		EPA, "Assessing and Managing Chemicals Under TSCA; The Frank R. Lautenberg Chemical Safety for the 21st Century Act"	https://www.epa.gov/assessing-and-managing-chemicals-under-tsca/frank-r-lautenberg-chemical-safety-21st-century-act
2.1.4	RCRA	EPA, "Summary of the Resource Conservation and Recovery Act"	https://www.epa.gov/laws-regulations/summary-resource-conservation-and-recovery-act
		EPA, "Resource Conservation and Recovery Act (RCRA) Overview"	https://www.epa.gov/rcra/resource-conservation-and-recovery-act-rcra-overview
2.1.5	CERCLA or Superfund	EPA, "Summary of the Comprehensive Environmental Response, Compensation, and Liability Act (Superfund)"	https://www.epa.gov/laws-regulations/summary-comprehensive-environmental-response-compensation-and-liability-act
		EPA, "Emergency Planning and Community Right-to-Know Act (EPCRA)"	https://www.epa.gov/epcra
2.2	Superfund — A Deeper Dive		
2.2.1	Site Assessment	EPA, "Superfund Site Assessment Process"	https://www.epa.gov/superfund/superfund-site-assessment-process
2.2.2	Placement on the NPL	EPA, "Basic NPL Information"	https://www.epa.gov/superfund/basic-npl-information
2.2.3	RI/FS	EPA, "Superfund Remedial Investigation/Feasibility Study (Site Characterization)"	https://www.epa.gov/superfund/superfund-remedial-investigationfeasibility-study-site-characterization
		U.S. Army Corps of Engineers Hazardous, Toxic, and Radioactive Waste Center of Expertise and EPA Office of Emergency and Remedial Response, *A Guide to Developing and Documenting Cost Estimates During the Feasibility Study*, July 2000	https://semspub.epa.gov/work/HQ/174890.pdf
2.2.4	Remediation Decisions	EPA Office of Solid Waste and Emergency Response (OSWER), *Rules of Thumb for Superfund Remedy Selection*, August 1997	https://semspub.epa.gov/work/HQ/174931.pdf
		FRTR, *Remediation Technologies Screening Matrix and Reference Guide*	https://frtr.gov/matrix2/section1/toc.html

(Table continued)

Section	Section Title	Source	URL
2.2.4.1.1	Soil Removal	EPA, *A Citizen's Guide to Excavation of Contaminated Soil*, September 2012	https://www.epa.gov/remedytech/citizens-guide-excavation-contaminated-soil
		Occupational Safety and Health Administration (OSHA) Technical Manual, TED 01-00-015, "Excavations: Hazard Recognition in Trenching and Shoring"	https://www.osha.gov/dts/osta/otm/otm_v/otm_v_2.html
		FRTR, *Remediation Technologies Screening Matrix and Reference Guide*	https://frtr.gov/matrix2/section1/toc.html
2.2.4.1.2	Soil Treatment and Stabilization	EPA, *In Situ Treatment Technologies for Contaminated Soil: Engineering Forum Issue Paper*, November 2006	https://www.epa.gov/remedytech/situ-treatment-technologies-contaminated-soil-engineering-forum-issue-paper
		EPA, "Remediation Technology Descriptions for Cleaning Up Contaminated Sites"	https://www.epa.gov/remedytech/remediation-technology-descriptions-cleaning-contaminated-sites
2.2.4.2.1	Ex Situ Groundwater Treatment	EPA, *A Citizen's Guide to Pump and Treat*, September 2012	https://www.epa.gov/remedytech/citizens-guide-pump-and-treat
		FRTR, "Common Treatment Technologies for Inorganics in Ground Water, Surface Water, and Leachate"	https://frtr.gov/matrix2/section2/2_8_3.html
		FRTR, "Ex Situ Physical/Chemical Treatment (Assuming Pumping): Granulated Activated Carbon (GAC)/Liquid Phase Carbon Adsorption"	https://frtr.gov/matrix2/section4/4-47.html
2.2.4.2.2	In Situ Groundwater Treatment	FRTR, "In Situ Physical/Chemical Treatment for Ground Water, Surface Water and Leachate"	https://frtr.gov/matrix2/section3/3_10.html
		EPA, *A Citizen's Guide to Pump and Treat*, September 2012	https://www.epa.gov/remedytech/citizens-guide-pump-and-treat
		FRTR, "In Situ Physical/Chemical Treatment: Air Sparging"	https://frtr.gov/matrix2/section4/4-34.html
		FRTR, "In Situ Physical/Chemical Treatment: Chemical Oxidation"	https://frtr.gov/matrix2/section4/4-30.html
		FRTR, "In Situ Physical/Chemical Treatment: Thermal Treatment"	https://frtr.gov/matrix2/section4/4-38.html
		FRTR, "In Situ Biological Treatment: Enhanced Bioremediation"	https://frtr.gov/matrix2/section4/4-31.html
		FRTR, "In Situ Biological Treatment: Phytoremediation"	https://frtr.gov/matrix2/section4/4-33.html

(Table continued)

Section	Section Title	Source	URL
2.2.4.2.2	In Situ Groundwater Treatment	EPA ORD, *Pump-and-Treat Ground-Water Remediation: A Guide for Decision Makers and Practitioners*, July 1996	https://nepis.epa.gov/Exe/ZyPDF.cgi/30004PC8.PDF?Dockey=30004PC8.pdf
		EPA OSWER, *A Citizen's Guide to Permeable Reactive Barriers*, September 2012	https://clu-in.org/download/Citizens/a_citizens_guide_to_permeable_reactive_barriers.pdf
		Interstate Technology & Regulatory Council (ITRC), *Permeable Reactive Barrier: Technology Update*, June 2011	https://www.itrcweb.org/GuidanceDocuments/PRB-5-1.pdf
2.2.4.2.3	Monitored Natural Attenuation	EPA OSWER, *A Citizen's Guide to Monitored Natural Attenuation*, September 2012	https://clu-in.org/download/Citizens/a_citizens_guide_to_monitored_natural_attenuation.pdf
		ITRC, *Permeable Reactive Barrier: Technology Update*, June 2011	https://www.itrcweb.org/GuidanceDocuments/PRB-5-1.pdf
		EPA ORD, *Technical Protocol for Evaluating Natural Attenuation of Chlorinated Solvents in Ground Water*, September 1998	https://clu-in.org/download/remed/protocol.pdf
2.2.4.2.4	Groundwater Containment	FRTR, "Ground Water, Surface Water, and Leachate: Containment: Physical Barriers"	https://frtr.gov/matrix2/section4/4-53.html
		Quintal, David and Otero, Margarita, "Vertical Impermeable Barriers (Cutoff Walls)," Geoengineer.org	https://www.geoengineer.org/education/web-based-class-projects/geoenvironmental-remediation-technologies/impermeable-barriers?showall=1&limitstart
		Indiana Department of Environmental Management, *Engineering Control: Slurry Walls*, April 1, 2013	https://www.in.gov/idem/landquality/files/risc_announce_20120328_engineered_controls_slurry_walls.pdf
2.2.4.2.5	Controlling Exposure to Contaminated Soil and Groundwater	Committee on Environmental Remediation at Naval Facilities et al., *Environmental Cleanup at Navy Facilities: Risk-Based Methods*, National Academy Press, 1999	https://www.nap.edu/catalog/6330/environmental-cleanup-at-navy-facilities-risk-based-methods
		EPA OSWER, *Engineering Controls on Brownfields Information Guide: How They Work With Institutional Controls; the Most Common Types Used; and an Introduction to Costs*, November 2010	https://www.epa.gov/sites/production/files/2015-09/documents/ec_information_guide.pdf
2.2.4.3	Sediment Remediation	EPA OSWER, *Contaminated Sediment Remediation Guidance for Hazardous Waste Sites*, December 2005	https://semspub.epa.gov/work/HQ/174471.pdf

(Table continued)

Section	Section Title	Source	URL
2.2.4.3.1	Dredging and Excavation	ITRC, *Contaminated Sediments Remediation: Remedy Selection for Contaminated Sediments*, August 2014	https://www.itrcweb.org/contseds_remedy-selection/
2.2.4.3.2	In Situ Techniques	See 2.2.4.3.1 above.	See 2.2.4.3.1 above.
2.2.4.3.3	Monitored Natural Recovery	See 2.2.4.3.1 above.	See 2.2.4.3.1 above.
2.2.6.1	OM&M	EPA OSWER, *Operation and Maintenance in the Superfund Program*, May 2001	https://semspub.epa.gov/work/HQ/176112.pdf
		U.S. Army Corps of Engineers Hazardous, Toxic, and Radioactive Waste Center of Expertise and EPA Office of Emergency and Remedial Response, *A Guide to Developing and Documenting Cost Estimates During the Feasibility Study*, July 2000	https://semspub.epa.gov/work/HQ/174890.pdf
2.2.6.2	Long-Term Response Action	EPA, "Superfund: Post Construction Completion"	https://www.epa.gov/superfund/superfund-post-construction-completion
2.2.6.3	Five-Year Reviews	EPA OSWER, *Five-Year Review Process in the Superfund Program*, April 2003	https://semspub.epa.gov/work/HQ/174760.pdf
2.2.6.4	Deletion From the NPL	EPA, "Superfund: NPL Deletion Guidance and Policy"	https://www.epa.gov/superfund/superfund-npl-deletion-guidance-and-policy
2.2.7	EPA "Notice of Liability" Letters to PRPs	EPA OSWER, "Interim Guidance on Notice Letters, Negotiations, and Information Exchange," October 19, 1987	https://www.epa.gov/enforcement/interim-guidance-notice-letters-negotiations-and-information-exchange
2.2.9	Superfund Settlement Agreements	See 2.2.7 above.	See 2.2.7 above.
2.3	Corrective Action Process Under RCRA	Rogers, C. Gregory, *Financial Reporting of Environmental Liabilities and Risks After Sarbanes-Oxley*, 2005, 48	
2.4	Environmental Regulations — State		
2.4.1	Federal-State Partnerships	Paddock, Leroy, *The Federal and State Roles in Environmental Enforcement: A Proposal for a More Effective and More Efficient Relationship*, Pace University DigitalCommons@Pace, January 1, 1990	https://digitalcommons.pace.edu/cgi/viewcontent.cgi?referer=&httpsredir=1&article=1234&context=lawfaculty
		Environmental Law Institute, "Environmental Law 101: Governance"	https://www.eli.org/keywords/governance

(Table continued)

Section	Section Title	Source	URL
2.4.1	Federal-State Partnerships	42 U.S.C. Section 7410, "State Implementation Plans for National Primary and Secondary Ambient Air Quality Standards"	https://www.gpo.gov/fdsys/granule/USCODE-2011-title42/USCODE-2011-title42-chap85-subchapI-partA-sec7410
		33 U.S.C. Section 1342(b), "National Pollutant Discharge Elimination System: State Permit Programs"	https://www.gpo.gov/fdsys/pkg/USCODE-1999-title33/pdf/USCODE-1999-title33-chap26-subchapIV-sec1342.pdf
		33 U.S.C. Section 1319(a), "Enforcement: State Enforcement; Compliance Orders"	https://www.gpo.gov/fdsys/pkg/USCODE-2016-title33/pdf/USCODE-2016-title33-chap26-subchapIII-sec1319.pdf
2.4.2	State Environmental Cleanup Regulations	30 Texas Administrative Code Section 350.55(e)(1)	http://txrules.elaws.us/rule/title30_chapter350_sec.350.55
		RCRA Sections 3004(u), 3004(v); 42 U.S.C. Sections 6924(u), 6924(v)	
2.4.3	Transaction-Triggered Environmental Laws	New Jersey Administrative Code Section 7:26	http://www.state.nj.us/dep/dshw/resource/rules.htm
		See 2.3 above.	
		Connecticut Department of Energy & Environmental Protection, "Property Transfer Program: An Environmental Program Fact Sheet"	http://www.ct.gov/DEep/cwp/view.asp?a=2715&q=325006&deepNav_GID=1626
		Delaware Code Title 7, Section 9201 et seq.	
2.4.4	Licensed Environmental Professionals	Miller, Kristen, "Connecticut Transfer Act," September 17, 2012	https://www.cga.ct.gov/2012/rpt/2012-R-0383.htm
		Massachusetts Department of Environmental Protection, 310 CMR 40, "Massachusetts Contingency Plan"	
		Mass.gov, "Hiring a Licensed Site Professional"	https://www.mass.gov/how-to/hiring-a-licensed-site-professional
		Farer, David B., "Transaction-Triggered Environmental Laws," Chapter 3 in *Environmental Aspects of Real Estate and Commercial Transactions*, edited by James Witkin, American Bar Association, 2011	
		Connecticut Department of Energy & Environmental Protection, "Licensed Environmental Professional Program: An Environmental Program Fact Sheet"	http://www.ct.gov/deep/cwp/view.asp?a=2715&q=324984&deepNav_GID=1626

(Table continued)

Section	Section Title	Source	URL
2.4.4	Licensed Environmental Professionals	Oberer, John, "Licensed Environmental Professionals: Do These Programs Work?" *New Jersey Business*, February 26, 2016	http://njbmagazine.com/special_sections/assessing-the-transition/licensed-environmental-professionals-do-these-programs-work/
2.4.5	Risk-Based Cleanup	National Academy of Sciences, "Review of Risk-Based Methodologies," Chapter 2 in *Environmental Cleanup at Navy Facilities: Risk-Based Methods*, National Academy Press, 1999	https://www.nap.edu/read/6330/chapter/4
		Oregon Department of Environmental Quality, *Risk-Based Decision Making for the Remediation of Contaminated Sites*, September 22, 2003	https://www.oregon.gov/deq/FilterDocs/RBDMGuidance.pdf
		Oklahoma Department of Environmental Quality, "Risk-Based Decision Making for Site Cleanup," July 2013	http://www.deq.state.ok.us/factsheets/land/SiteCleanUp.pdf
		ITRC, *Contaminated Sediments Remediation: Remedy Selection for Contaminated Sediments*, August 2014	https://clu-in.org/download/contaminantfocus/sediments/Sediment-ITRC-CS-2.pdf
		Downey, Douglas et al., "Trends in Regulatory Acceptance of Risk-Based Cleanup Goals and Natural Attenuation for Site Closure," *Remediation: The Journal of Environmental Cleanup Costs, Technologies & Techniques*, December 1997, 71–86	http://citrix.ngwa.org/gwol/pdf/960162453.pdf
2.5	Environmental Regulations — International	Sands, Philippe and Peel, Jacqueline, *Principles of International Environmental Law*, third edition, Cambridge University Press, 2012	http://www.cambridge.org/gb/academic/subjects/law/environmental-law/principles-international-environmental-law-3rd-edition?format=HB&isbn=9780521769594#Xh9tCf2JC8qTIEWY.97
		Secretariat of the Basel, Rotterdam, and Stockholm Conventions, "Synergies Among the Basel, Rotterdam, and Stockholm Conventions: First Intergovernmental Environment Meetings After UNEA2 Conclude With Concrete Steps Taken to Manage More Sustainability"	http://www.brsmeas.org/Implementation/MediaResources/PressReleases/1stIntergovEnvMeetings/tabid/5193/language/en-US/Default.aspx
		See 2.3 above.	

(Table continued)

Section	Section Title	Source	URL
2.5	Environmental Regulations — International	European Commission, "Environmental Liability"	http://ec.europa.eu/environment/legal/liability/index.htm
		Kadas, Madeleine and Fraker, Russell, "Central and South America Overview: Emerging Trends in Latin America," *International Environmental Law: The Practitioner's Guide to the Laws of the Planet*, edited by Roger Martella, Jr. and J. Brett Grosko, American Bar Association, 2014, 365, 368–369	http://www.bdlaw.com/assets/attachments/419.pdf
5.3	Power and Utilities — Nuclear		
5.3.3	High-Level Radioactive Waste	NRC, "Backgrounder on Decommissioning Nuclear Power Plants"	https://www.nrc.gov/reading-rm/doc-collections/fact-sheets/decommissioning.html
		DOE, *Strategy for the Management and Disposal of Used Nuclear Fuel and High-Level Radioactive Waste*, January 2013	https://www.energy.gov/em/downloads/strategy-management-and-disposal-used-nuclear-fuel-and-high-level-radioactive-waste
		DOE Office of Civilian Radioactive Waste Management, Office of Scientific and Technical Information, *Acceptance Priority Ranking & Annual Capacity Report*, 2004	https://www.osti.gov/biblio/1185215-acceptance-priority-ranking-annual-capacity-report
5.4	Power and Utilities — Non-Nuclear		
5.4.1	Coal Ash Impoundments	CFR Parts 257 and 261, "Hazardous and Solid Waste Management System; Disposal of Coal Combustion Residuals From Electric Utilities — EPA Final Rule"	https://www.gpo.gov/fdsys/pkg/FR-2015-04-17/pdf/2015-00257.pdf

Appendix C — Titles of Standards and Other Literature

The following are the titles of standards and other literature mentioned in this publication:

AICPA Statement of Position
96-1, *Environmental Remediation Liabilities*

Environmental Protection Agency (EPA) Rule
Disposal of Coal Combustion Residuals From Electric Utilities (the "CCR rule")

FASB Accounting Standards Codification (ASC) Topics
ASC 205, *Presentation of Financial Statements*

ASC 210, *Balance Sheet*

ASC 235, *Notes to Financial Statements*

ASC 250, *Accounting Changes and Error Corrections*

ASC 275, *Risks and Uncertainties*

ASC 360, *Property, Plant, and Equipment*

ASC 410, *Asset Retirement and Environmental Obligations*

ASC 450, *Contingencies*

ASC 805, *Business Combinations*

ASC 820, *Fair Value Measurement*

ASC 835, *Interest*

ASC 840, *Leases*

ASC 842, *Leases*

ASC 855, *Subsequent Events*

ASC 932, *Extractive Activities — Oil and Gas*

FASB Accounting Standards Update (ASU)
ASU 2016-02, *Leases (Topic 842)*

FASB Statements (Pre-Codification Literature)

No. 143, *Accounting for Asset Retirement Obligations*

No. 5, *Accounting for Contingencies*

FASB Interpretation (Pre-Codification Literature)

Interpretation No. 47, *Accounting for Conditional Asset Retirement Obligations* — an interpretation of FASB Statement No. 143

Accounting Research Bulletin (Pre-Codification Literature)

No. 22, *Disclosure of Accounting Policies*

SEC Regulation S-K

Item 101, "Description of Business"

Item 103, "Legal Proceedings"

Item 303, "Management's Discussion and Analysis of Financial Condition and Results of Operations"

SEC Staff Accounting Bulletin (SAB)

SAB Topic 5.Y, "Accounting and Disclosures Relating to Loss Contingencies"

International Standards

IAS 16, *Property, Plant and Equipment*

IAS 37, *Provisions, Contingent Liabilities and Contingent Assets*

IFRIC Interpretation 1, *Changes in Existing Decommissioning, Restoration and Similar Liabilities*

Appendix D — Abbreviations

Abbreviation	Description
ACM	asbestos-containing material
AICPA	American Institute of Certified Public Accountants
AMD	acid mine drainage
AOC	administrative order on consent
APB	FASB Accounting Principles Board
ARAR	applicable or relevant and appropriate requirement
ARO	asset retirement obligation
ASC	FASB Accounting Standards Codification
ASU	FASB Accounting Standards Update
CCR	coal combustion residual
CD	consent decree
CFR	U.S. Code of Federal Regulations
CMI	Corrective Measures Implementation
CMS	Corrective Measures Study
COC	contaminant of concern
DECON	immediate dismantling, one of three options for nuclear decommissioning
DNAPL	dense non-aqueous phase liquid
DOE	U.S. Department of Energy
DOJ	U.S. Department of Justice
EITF	Emerging Issues Task Force
EMNR	enhanced monitored natural recovery
ENTOMB	permanent encasing (entombing), one of three options for nuclear decommissioning

Abbreviation	Description
EPA	U.S. Environmental Protection Agency
EU	European Union
FASB	Financial Accounting Standards Board
FRTR	Federal Remediation Technologies Roundtable
FS	feasibility study
FYR	five-year review
GAAP	generally accepted accounting principles
HRS	Hazard Ranking System
IAS	International Accounting Standard
IFRIC	International Financial Reporting Interpretations Committee
IFRS	International Financial Reporting Standard
ISFSI	independent spent fuel storage installation
ITRC	Interstate Technology & Regulatory Council
LEP	licensed environmental professional
LNAPL	light non-aqueous phase liquid
LSP	licensed site professional
LSRP	licensed site remediation professional
LTP	license termination plan
LTRA	long-term response action
MassDEP	Massachusetts Department of Environmental Protection
MCL	maximum contaminant level

Abbreviation	Description
MD&A	Management's Discussion and Analysis
MGP	manufactured gas plant
MNA	monitored natural attenuation
MNR	monitored natural recovery
MTBE	methyl tert-butyl ether
NAPL	non-aqueous phase liquid
NFA	no further action
NJDEP	New Jersey Department of Environmental Protection
NPDES	National Pollutant Discharge Elimination System
NPL	National Priorities List
NO_x	nitrogen oxides
NRC	U.S. Nuclear Regulatory Commission
OM&M	operations, maintenance, and monitoring
ORD	EPA Office of Research and Development
OSWER	EPA Office of Solid Waste and Emergency Response
PAH	polyaromatic hydrocarbon
PCB	polychlorinated biphenyl
PCC	postclosure care
PCE	perchloroethylene
PRB	permeable reactive barrier
PRP	potentially responsible party
PSDAR	post-shutdown activities report
RAO	response action outcome
RD/RA	remedial design/remedial action
RFI	RCRA Facility Investigation
RI	remedial investigation
ROD	record of decision
SAB	SEC Staff Accounting Bulletin
SAFSTOR	deferred dismantling, one of three options for nuclear decommissioning

Abbreviation	Description
SEC	Securities and Exchange Commission
SO_2	sulfur dioxide
SVOC	semivolatile organic compound
Syngas	synthetic gas
TCE	trichloroethylene
TCEQ	Texas Commission on Environmental Quality
UAO	unilateral administrative order
VCP	voluntary cleanup program
VOC	volatile organic compound

The following is a list of short references for the Acts and legislation mentioned in this publication:

Abbreviation	Description
CAA	Clean Air Act of 1970
CERCLA	Comprehensive Environmental Response, Compensation, and Liability Act of 1980
CWA	Clean Water Act of 1972
EPCRA	Emergency Planning and Community Right-to-Know Act
HSWA	Federal Hazardous and Solid Waste Amendments
ISRA	New Jersey Industrial Site Recovery Act
MCP	Massachusetts Contingency Plan
NAAQS	National Ambient Air Quality Standards
NCP	National Oil and Hazardous Substances Pollution Contingency Plan
RCRA	Resource Conservation and Recovery Act of 1976
SARA	Superfund Amendments and Reauthorization Act of 1986
SMCRA	Surface Mining Control and Reclamation Act
TRRP	Texas Risk Reduction Program
TSCA	Toxic Substances Control Act of 1976

Made in the USA
Lexington, KY
05 August 2018